There are in the world valleys which are larger and a few which are deeper. There are valleys flanked by summits loftier than the palisades of the Kaibab. Still the Grand Canyon is the sublimest thing on earth. It is so not alone by virtue of its magnitude, but by virtue of the whole — its ensemble.

CLARENCE E. DUTTON

SIERRA CLUB EXHIBIT FORMAT SERIES

Winner of the Carey-Thomas Award in 1964
for the best achievement in creative publishing in the United States

EDITED BY DAVID BROWER

Titles marked *, and the following, are available
as Sierra Club-Ballantine paperbacks:
  Sierra Club Wilderness Handbook, edited by David Brower
  The Population Bomb, by Dr. Paul R. Ehrlich
  Manual of Ski Mountaineering, edited by David Brower
  On the Loose, by Terry & Renny Russell

GRAND CANYON OF
THE LIVING COLORADO

When you think of the Grand Canyon, what comes to your mind?
Do you think of being in it, or gliding by the great rock walls
that mark off an immensity of space for the spirit to soar through?

Do you think of the widening of the space as seeps dissolve
the old limestone and tributaries wear away the still older sandstone?

Do you think of the living river, basic to all,
as it deepens the Canyon, gouging and scouring its way
through rock transfigured by two billion years of heat and weight?

Do you think of the water bringing the elements of life to each canyon garden?
. . . of the plants, growing in the sand,
pointing up the subtle color of the rocks,
contrasting delicately with the seeming harshness of the Canyon?

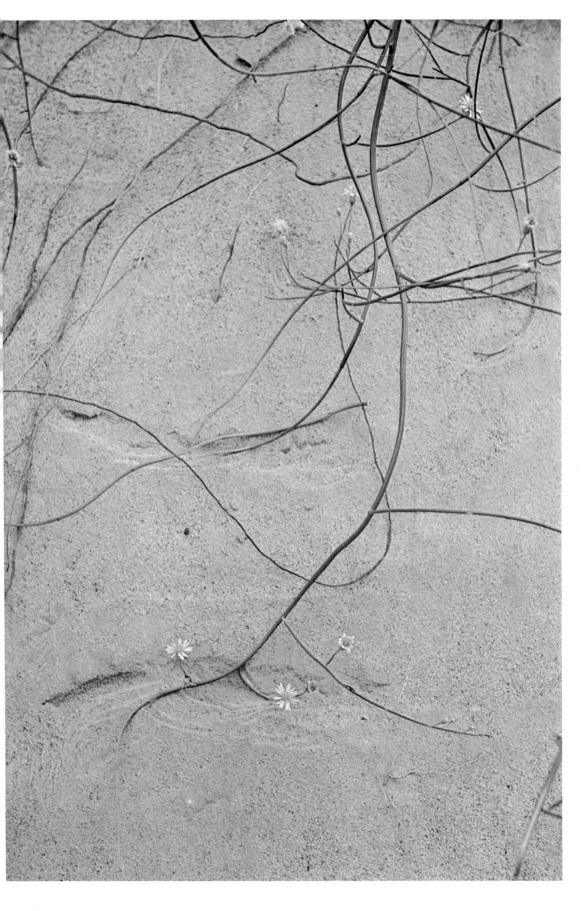

Do you think of exploring to find out what the Canyon has tucked away?

Do you think of riding its river, urged and tugged
by the power of its current, challenging, magic, alive?

GRAND CANYON
OF THE LIVING COLORADO

Photographs and a journal by ERNEST BRAUN

Contributions by COLIN FLETCHER, ALLEN J. MALMQUIST,
RODERICK NASH, and STEWART L. UDALL

*With excerpts from the narration by David Brower, Jeffrey Ingram, and Martin Litton
for the Sierra Club film "The Grand Canyon" accompanying the color plates*

Edited by RODERICK NASH
Foreword by DAVID BROWER

SIERRA CLUB · BALLANTINE BOOKS

The Sierra Club, founded in 1892 by the Scotsman John Muir, has devoted itself to the study and protection of scenic resources and wild things, and to acting in behalf of people who cannot live without either, now and in the future. The club is affiliated with the International Union for Conservation, the Natural Resources Council of America, The Appalachian Trail Conference, and the Federation of Western Outdoor Clubs. Sierra Club chapters embrace most of the United States and part of Canada. Participation is invited in the club's program. Sierra Club publications are part of the nonprofit effort the club carries on as a public trust.

Addresses: San Francisco 94104, Mills Tower (main office)
New York 10019, 250 West 57th Street
Washington, D. C. 20002, 235 Massachusetts Avenue, N. E.
Albuquerque 87106, 111D Harvard Drive, S. E.
Los Angeles 90013, Auditorium Building
Seattle 98105, 4534½ University Way, N. E.

Paperback edition, Ballentine Books, 101 Fifth Avenue, New York 10003

This book is set in Fairfield by Gillick Printing, Berkeley
The color is lithographed by Barnes Press, New York
Production is by Heliographic Co., New York

FOREWORD

INTANGIBLES, such as the meaning of a wild Grand Canyon, are hard to talk about but too important to the world to ignore. The marketplace cannot measure them usefully until it learns how to tell us what it would cost to build a separate but equal Grand Canyon. Marketplaces cannot inform us about many vital things, such as love for people or for environment. Man's humanity lags behind his technology—one explanation for the hydrogen bomb. Until the lag ends there will be threats to the Canyon.

We have been changing our environment with accelerating technological speed, hardly pausing to weigh ecological consequences. Although we know little about what tools man used for his first million years, we have learned that for the 300,000 years thereafter he managed with no tool more complicated than a shaped stone, which he learned to attach a stick to and then to decorate. It did little harm to the environment, which reciprocated by not striking back. One good tool, however, led to another, and to the technological spurt that has been with us about two centuries. The cost of the resulting successes in environmental engineering is still subject to audit. We suspect that the price is too high as we find less and less natural world around us, a shortage of good water and air, and fewer places of beauty to nourish spirit. We realize the implications of our own ever-increasing numbers. We perceive that we are of nature, not above it—that because of our power we must exercise stewardship for other life forms. We comprehend Aldo Leopold's "ecological conscience" and his "land ethic."

Or at least we ought to. But man's ability to control tools has not caught up with his ability to fashion them. The conservation movement, born to close this gap, assumes that man is in the dawn of a culture, not its dusk: the resources we have presently, including the vestigial resources of unspoiled and beautiful environment, must last for all the centuries to come; the wilderness we have now is all we will ever have. The first imperative is that we bequeath a freedom of choice, one of those freedoms being the chance to see unspoiled wilderness, or simply to know that it exists, and to know that it exists spectacularly in places like the Grand Canyon. Much more than wilderness is at stake.

The prime movers of this book are lovers of the Canyon. Martin Litton, pilot, photographer, writer, editor, and Sierra Club director, first ran the Colorado River in the 1950s, when only about 180 men had ever done it. He has run it often since, and his skills as boatman and guide have been a major part of the Sierra Club's effort on behalf of the Canyon. The gaily painted double-prowed dories of his own design have carried him to legendary status on the river; the force of his conviction has carried the river's value to millions. It is one thing to love beautiful places. It is another to act forcibly to save them. He does.

On one of his trips I met Ernest Braun. Preoccupied with looking into finders myself, and at oncoming rapids and outgoing side canyons, I failed to notice that Mr. Braun was working harder with his own cameras and journal. Later, I saw enlargements of his 35mm color and knew that nothing less than some traveling exhibits and this book would do to bring his perception of Grand Canyon to the crusade for a greater Grand Canyon National Park. Mr. Braun is a photographer of extraordinary ability, and when his subjects are in action he is willing to spend a roll—of film or boat— to capture one glorious moment.

Jeffrey Ingram, the Sierra Club's Southwest Representative, was on that river trip too. Like Mr. Braun, he took sensitive emulsion to his Canyon voyage. His impressions figured prominently in the club's color motion picture made to help save the Canyon as well as in his testimony, before Congress and elsewhere, in the course of his contribution to the campaign to defeat the dams. He was one of the three M.I.T. graduates (Laurence I. Moss, nuclear engineer, and Alan Carlin, economist, were the others) who put technology to the aid of environment in the Congressional hearings. In his mathematician's analysis he separated the alleged income of the proposed dams from the real income of existing dams below Lake Mead, demonstrating to Congressional committees and the Bureau of the Budget a major fallacy in the Bureau of Reclamation's proposal for damming Grand Canyon. Excerpts from the narration of the film he produced (and Martin Litton photographed) complement this book's illustrations.

An explorer of history as well as of country, Roderick Nash first confronted the Canyon as an eleven-year-old when he backpacked from rim to rim. He has returned often, most recently to run the river in neoprene rafts and a seven-foot kayak. Dr. Nash is author of a prize-winning book, *Wilderness and the American Mind,* and of *The American Environment: Readings in the History of Conservation.* We coaxed him from his duties as a professor at the University of California, Santa Barbara, long enough to knit this volume together.

We hope that what exposure to Grand Canyon has done to these people will help other people know that it takes a living river to keep a canyon alive. "And finer forms are in the quarry/ Than ever Angelo evoked." They will continue to be exposed in the Canyon as long as time and the river keep flowing.

DAVID BROWER

CONTENTS

THE BACKPACKER'S CANYON

Going on foot is the only way to get close to the Grand Canyon between the rims and the river. Many hike the spectacular Bright Angel trail from the national park center on the South Rim to the river and Phantom Ranch, sharing the right-of-way with the popular mule trains. Less frequented is the Kaibab Trail on which one can walk from rim to rim, crossing the Colorado on a narrow suspension bridge. A few hike or ride the trails from Hualapai or Topocoba Hilltop to the Havasupai Indian Reservation at the western edge of the national park. The rest of Grand Canyon, and there are thousands of square miles of it, is known only to a handful of "pros": wild burros, desert bighorn sheep, mountain lions, and bold, skilled walkers like Allen J. Malmquist and Colin Fletcher. Here they describe their adventures in the back country of Grand Canyon, much of which is not at present a part of Grand Canyon National Park.—ED.

Exploring the Western Grand Canyon

ALLEN J. MALMQUIST

THE WESTERN two-thirds of Grand Canyon is a vast, forgotten wilderness. On the map, it appears as a hundred-mile-wide blank space west of Grand Canyon National Park. Such was not the case around the turn of the century. Ranchers, cattlemen, Indians, and prospectors lived there at various levels from rim to river. Tourists reached the rims by horse and wagon, and explored the inner canyon on an extensive network of trails. Aerial trams crossed the river. Bridge Canyon City, Quartermaster and Meriwhitica Springs, Diamond Canyon, the Shivwits Plateau, Havasu Canyon, and Bass Camp were some of the places actively developed.

Yet few of these enterprises were successful. As national advertising focused all attention on the resorts in the new park at the east end of the Canyon, the other areas became deserted; the trails and access roads were abandoned, and the western two-thirds of Grand Canyon were soon forgotten. Its deep, narrow gorges, broad plateaus, streams, and oases are only now being rediscovered as unique in their own right, equaling anything in the national park.

One route that explores the very heart of this wilderness is the old trail to Bridge Canyon City. Sixty miles west of the park, a series of primitive jeep roads crosses the Hualapai Indian Reservation through a maze of plateaus and canyons to viewpoints along the south rim. At the head of Bridge Canyon, the old horse trail descends a narrow fault that is the only break in the rim cliff for over 20 miles. A well-beaten path follows the route down the slot, as it is the only passage for deer and wild burros from their grazing land on the rim to their drinking water in the gorge below.

As with most old canyon trails, short stretches of the upper part of this one are washed out, covered by rock slides, and overgrown with brush. Yet the switchbacks down the cliff and talus are obvious and readily passable for any cautious hiker.

Out on the broad floor of the upper canyon, the trail soon peters out and the hiker is on his own for awhile. But there is no sense of isolation as one is not alone. There can be quite a bit of activity at the upper spring. After a chorus of loud braying that echoes off the cliffs, a dozen or more wild burros often come racing to the water as if playing some game. They are surprised at finding the hiker there, yet curious enough to follow the intruder down the wash. These animals are the descendants of burros abandoned by prospectors years ago. The burros have multiplied until they now roam the whole length of Grand Canyon.

Bridge Canyon is actually only a deep indentation in the south rim of Grand Canyon. It is less than four miles from the huge amphitheater at its head to the river, deep in the inner gorge. Grand Canyon is incredibly narrow in this area. The only break in the 3,500-foot Redwall cliffs that form the north and south rims is a quarter-mile-wide plateau running along the middle of the Canyon above the Lower Granite Gorge. The inner gorge is a deep trough cut into ancient black granites, and contains the Colorado River itself. This terrain contrasts with the ten-mile-wide sections of the Canyon in the park, where a whole series of cliffs and plateaus terraces down to the river.

Bridge Canyon Wash begins dropping into the inner gorge only three miles from the rim. But waterfalls down in its narrow, twisting channel make it impractical to reach the river here, so the trail turns out onto the plateau and makes its way down the Colorado above the gorge. It is six miles before there is a place where a trail could be easily built down to the river.

Nevertheless, hikers can continue down to the mouth of Bridge Canyon. A climb down the side of a waterfall brings one into an intimate little glen full of willows and redbud. A series of springs have formed a clear rushing stream full of watercress. Seeps and maidenhair ferns decorate the walls. Scarlet monkey flowers, columbines, and tamarisk are alive with butterflies and hummingbirds. Nearby is the natural bridge that gives the area its name. Croaking gray frogs compete with the rumble of Bridge Canyon Rapids, a quarter-mile away. This oasis is alive and vibrant. One gets a real feeling for what would be lost if this area were to be flooded by the proposed Hualapai (formerly Bridge Canyon) dam.

Rejoining the trail up on the plateau, one continues toward Bridge Canyon City. The trail is in good condition where it detours around the head of each side canyon, but often disappears crossing the flat areas along the edge of the gorge.

This plateau is home for a variety of small animals. Ground squirrels, mice, lizards, cottontails, jacks, and even gophers are seen busy in the shade of the rabbitbrush and sage.

After rounding the head of Gneiss Canyon, the trail goes out onto the edge of the gorge above Hualapai damsite. This area is the most spectacular part of the Lower Granite Gorge. The river has cut a narrow slot 700 feet deep through very resistant granite. Vertical walls of the dark rock rise from the water, gleaming in the sun where they have been polished by high floods. This is where dam builders hope to plug Grand Canyon with a mass of concrete 700 feet high. To destroy this spot would be a scenic loss in itself, to say nothing of the 93 miles of inner gorge and innumerable side canyons that would be flooded as far upstream as Kanab Canyon.

Six miles from Bridge Canyon the trail finally leaves the plateau and descends a steep fault zone to ruins beside the river. Stone foundations and twisted lumber are all that remain of Bridge Canyon City. A little bit of beach makes a good campsite beside the water, a narrow channel with no rapids, strangely silent. The river rushes along with only a gurgle from deep in the funnel of a whirlpool, or the sudden splash of an upswell.

One of the most popular hikes into the wilderness of the western Grand Canyon is the 35-mile trip down Kanab Canyon. Kanab Creek's headwaters are in the high plateaus of southern Utah, and the creek flows directly south 100 miles before joining the Colorado deep in Grand Canyon. Mormon pioneers built several trails off the north rim in this area, and some are still used by cattlemen with grazing rights in the lower canyons. One of these, the Hack Canyon Trail, provides excellent access to Kanab Canyon only 30 miles from the river.

The trailhead on the rim of Hack Canyon is unmarked and difficult to locate. The trail itself quickly descends the cliffs and ends as soon as it reaches the lower talus. It is only four miles to the junction of Hack Canyon and Kanab Canyon.

The Kanab is wide, dry, and full of cows. Only scattered cottonwoods and willows remain from the time when the canyon bottom was lined with trees. The creek has been diverted to irrigate farms up in Fredonia, and the resulting low water table, plus overgrazing and general drought, has hurt the canyon. There are acres of dead mesquite trees on dusty flats above the wash, and summer floods rush down the wide channel unchecked. Hikers often face a dry camp the first night out, as the creek is very unpredictable. A muddy trickle may flow after a spring storm, but it dries up completely within a few days. The cattle are rather wild and run from people. Often a hiker finds himself pushing a small herd down the canyon in spite of all attempts to avoid disturbing them.

The walls get higher as the creek works its way down through the red, orange, and brown Supai sandstones and finally deep into the Redwall limestone. Small side canyons entering Kanab Canyon provide excellent side trips. Most are blocked by dry falls, but a few, such as Davis and Swapps, can be followed to their heads and up onto the Esplanade—a huge, flat plateau several miles wide beneath the rim cliffs. One can hike along it for miles if he knows the exact location of all the water holes and springs.

Kanab Canyon is soon over 800 feet deep. At one sharp bend it loops back on itself, isolating a thin fin of rock 400 feet high called Scotty's Tower, after a local horse thief who hid stolen stock near here. The tower is stained with dark purple desert varnish, but the undercut cliff on the outside of the bend is brilliant white where huge sheets of limestone have flaked off into the streambed. A field of house-sized boulders makes this the most arduous mile of the trip.

Tracks of desert bighorn sheep become quite common in the mud and sand of the wash. The sheep are occasionally seen grazing on a steep slope or drinking from a pothole.

The last five miles become increasingly spectacular. At places the walls are only forty feet apart and over a thousand feet high. Nowhere else in Grand Canyon is there such a gorge. Sunlight hitting a distant cliff face seems to set it on fire, reflecting a golden glow into the shadowed recesses below. Straight up, the thin strip of pure blue sky adds to the riot of color.

The cliffs are streaked by seeps that water the hanging gardens of red monkey flowers, columbine, and maidenhair fern. Larger springs flow out of cracks in the walls and several have deposited thick canopies of travertine that arch out over the stream bed. The creek soon becomes quite large, and carp and trout are seen in the deeper pools. Side streams cascade over high falls or emerge from narrow breaks in the walls. These steep-sided canyons conceal dark, cool recesses, chutes, plunge pools, and impassable jumps.

After two and a half days of hiking, one is suddenly out on the beach beside the Colorado River beside Kanab Rapids—at the head of proposed Hualapai reservoir, 93 miles above the damsite.

A hike from rim to river is one of the supreme experiences in Grand Canyon. But a few words of caution are necessary. The Canyon is hospitable only to those who learn its special problems. Get the free booklet, "Inner Canyon Hiking," from the Superintendent of Grand Canyon National Park, and try one of the maintained trails in the park before attempting any of the old routes elsewhere.

Don't underestimate the climb out of the Canyon. Especially avoid doing it in the heat of the day. Many climb out at night by flashlight, but only if they are *positive* of the route. Leave water and food (canned fruits, etc.) at several places on the way down to have on the climb out. Learn to locate the route far in advance, as temporary loss of way is common.

It can be suicide to enter the Canyon in summer. Temperatures often reach 120°, and the dehydration can be so great that one cannot take in water as fast as it is sweated away. April is by far the best month for hiking, but late snows can still close the rim in places.

Hikers rarely meet anyone in the western Grand Canyon, and rescue is difficult if there is trouble. You are completely on your own—one of the strongest reasons for being there.

These two hikes typify the rewards of exploring western Grand Canyon *outside* of Grand Canyon National Park and National Monument. To gain knowledge of this wilderness is a lifelong endeavor—an endeavor that can continue as long as the river and its canyons remain wild and free.

The Man Who Walked Through Time

Colin Fletcher

It HAPPENED quite unexpectedly, the way the big moments often do. A friend and I were driving from New York to the West Coast in early June, and we had detoured north from US 66 for a hurried look at Grand Canyon. It was midmorning when we parked the car and walked across asphalt toward the Rim. I had seen my quota of photographs and paintings, of course, and thought I knew what to expect: an impressive view that no self-respecting tourist ought to miss.

Long before we came close, I saw the space. A huge, cleaving space that the photographs and paintings had done nothing to prepare me for. An impossible, breath-taking gap in the face of the earth. And up from this void shone a soft, luminous light.

We came to the lip of the Rim.

And there, defeating my senses, was the depth. The depth and the distances. Cliffs and buttes and hanging terraces, all sculptured on a scale beyond anything I had ever imagined. Colors neither red nor white nor pink nor purple but a fusion. And stamped across everything, the master pattern.

Even before I had accepted what I saw, I heard the silence; felt it, like something solid, face to face. A silence in which the squawk of a blue jay was sacrilege. A silence so profound that the whole colossal chaos of rock and space and color seemed to have sunk beneath it and to lie there cut off, timeless.

In the first moment of shock, with my mind already exploding beyond old boundaries, I knew that something had happened to the way I looked at things.

Oddly enough, I am no longer quite sure when the decision came. It was not, I know, during that first morning. But all afternoon I sat on the Rim and looked down into the burning and apparently waterless waste of rock. Looked more closely now at the master pattern that is the fabric of the Canyon. At the layered, sawtooth pattern that had leaped out at me, simple and striking, in that first moment of shock. I looked at its huge, alternating bands of cliff and hanging terrace that reach down, repeating but never repetitious, from Rim almost to river. I looked east and west, as far as my eyes could strain, until cliff and terrace tapered away into hazy distances. It was mysterious and terrible—and beckoning. And some time during the afternoon, as I sat on the brink of this strange new world, it came to me that if a route existed I would walk from one end of the Canyon to the other. Once the idea had crystallized, no hideously sensible doubts reared up to plague me. And I did not need such fragile props as "reasons." The only question I asked myself was whether the project would turn out to be physically possible. Perhaps it is in this kind of simple certainty that most of the world's ridiculous and wonderful dreams are born.

Late in the afternoon of that first day I went to the National Park Visitor Center. There I learned that although many people had run the river in boats, no one seemed to have forced a passage of the Canyon on foot. I was still aware, I think, only of the physical challenge of what I had seen, and the questions I asked were severely practical. I wanted to know, for example, whether it was possible for a man to make his way along those steep hanging terraces. (I have called them hanging terraces because that was how they immediately struck me; but perhaps I should explain that they are narrow, steeply sloping ledges that often extend for mile after mile after mile as precarious steps between successive cliff faces.) I also wanted to know whether water existed, here and there, down in that world of heat and dryness. But beyond the fact that people had died of thirst there, even in recent years, the only important thing I found out for certain was that nobody seemed to know very much about such matters. Yet as I strolled around the Visitor Center and studied its exhibits and talked to park rangers I learned many new facts. I learned about the vegetation that grows down in what your eye reports from the Rim as a wasteland of bare rock. (It is only distance that has canceled the signs of life.) I learned about the many animals that live in that "dead" world: not only spiders and rattlesnakes, but deer and coyotes and bobcats and even mountain lions. I learned about the fossils, those messages from the ancient past. About the rocks. And about their meanings. And after a while, reaching out at last beyond mere information, I grasped that the Canyon is a huge natural museum of the earth's history.

That evening I escaped from the crowded places—from the asphalt and its automobiles, from tourists harnessed to their cameras, from hotel porters in garish red jackets—and walked along an unfrequented stretch of the Rim. I sat down under a juniper tree. And in that quiet place I found that I had moved inside the silence.

When I had sat and looked for a long time at the tremendous expanse of rock sculpture spread out below me, I began to understand, more than just intellectually, something of how it had become sculpture. And I began to understand that the silence was not, as I had thought, a timeless silence. It was a silence built of the seconds that had ticked away, eon after eon, as certainly and deliberately as our seconds tick past today. Just for a moment I glimpsed the centuries reaching back and down into the Canyon and into the past, back and down through the corridor of time that stretches silently away behind us, back and down into the huge history that seems at first to leave no meaningful place for man.

And presently, when the fear had begun to subside, I saw that my decision to walk through the Canyon could mean more than I knew. I saw that by going down into that huge fissure in the face of the earth, deep into the space and the silence and the solitude, I might come as close as we can at present to moving back and down through the smooth and apparently impenetrable face of time. If I could contribute enough, the journey might teach me in the end, with a certainty no book can give, how the centuries have built the world we know. For I would see how the rocks had been constructed, and how they had been carved. How life had mushroomed from simple beginnings into the complex and astonishing pageant we now accept so casually. How it had covered the rocks with a web whose intricate and interlocking structure all too often becomes invisible to us "civilized" and estranged people. I would see many strands from this web: simple algae and lichens as well as juniper trees; catfish and butterflies and hummingbirds as well as wild horses and bighorn sheep and other members of that mammalian strand of life which has recently come to dominate the world's fabric. I would even find traces of the self-conscious mammal that has, for the last little cupful of centuries, multiplied its numbers and its complexities so prodigiously that it threatens, any minute now, to tear apart the whole delicately balanced structure and leave only tattered remnants trembling in the winds of time. I might even glimpse some hint of how this curious animal fits meaningfully into the broader scheme. I might find—beyond our present intellectual answers, but in harmony with them—some kind of new personal solution to man's ancient and continuing conundrums: "Where do we come from?" "What are we doing here?" For by living close to the web of life and to the foundations across which it stretches I might in the end gain some tentative insight into the pattern on which both have been built.

I did not understand, there under the juniper tree, how this vision would fit into my own small life. But it did not matter. I understood enough.

A year passed before I could start my journey.

Perhaps it was just as well: there is no test quite like the erosion of time for finding out whether you really want to do something. If the dream you have dreamed can survive untarnished through a year of doubt and discouragement and frustration and all the drawn-out detail of research and planning and preparation, then you can safely assume that you want to go through with the project. . . .

As the months passed I harvested all the practical information I could raise. It was a thin crop. I found, with one notable exception, no one who could help me very much. But I consulted excellent topographical maps, fairly complete weather statistics, and a couple of marginally informative old exploration reports. And slowly I found my outline answers.

I would set aside two months for the journey. I knew that I could probably force a passage through the Canyon considerably faster, but to do so would mean making my journey a battle. And what I wanted, if I could manage it, was something closer to a picnic. Or perhaps I mean a pilgrimage.

As I had expected, the obvious route along the Colorado was almost certainly out: the river often cut, mile after mile, through deep gorges that everyone agreed were impassable on foot. But the hanging terraces sometimes broadened into rock platforms, and even where they pinched into steep and narrow talus (a sloping mass of loose rock fragments), it seemed probable that in most places a man could pick his way along them.

The big barrier, I confirmed, was water. In the park's eastern half I would often be able to get down quite easily to the Colorado. There were also several permanent sidecreeks. But in the western section the river ran through an almost continuous gorge, rarely accessible from above, and I would have to rely mostly on rainpockets—small rockpools of rain or melted snow. Heavy rainshowers usually fell in late summer, but they were extremely erratic, and by then temperatures deep in the Canyon would on most days be over 100 degrees in the shade. A more reliable time for rain or snow was winter and early spring. But winter temperatures might fall almost as low as the 22 degrees below zero once recorded on the South Rim, and that is no weather for a pilgrimage, let alone a picnic. So I decided to start in early April. It seemed to me that if I planned efficiently, carried two gallons of water, did nothing foolish, and studiously avoided bad luck, I ought to get by.

I knew that even with a sixty-pound load on my back I could carry only one week's food at a time, so I decided to send one week's supply down by mule train to the Indian village of Supai, and other week's to Phantom Ranch, the only other inhabited place in the Canyon. I would also plant out two caches. And I would charter three parachute airdrops.

The supplies for both caches and drops would be packed in five-gallon metal cans. In addition to a week's dehydrated rations (spiced by one can of delicacies, such as oysters or frogs' legs, and a small bottle of claret) each can would contain such vital replacements as white gas for the cooking stove, toilet paper, book-matches, film, flashlight batteries, detergent powder, soap (half a bar), boot wax, onionskin paper for notes, rubbing alcohol for refreshing and hardening feet, and spare plastic freezer bags in various sizes for protecting almost everything. Some cans would also include socks, foot powder, and water-purifying tablets.

In the final month of the year of waiting, with preparations mounting to their inevitable climax, every day pulsated with problems: Grappling with the huge, multiple-minuscule issues of what equipment to take and what to leave behind. Deciding what to do about such hazards as rattlesnakes, scorpions, and twisted ankles miles from water. Discovering desperately late in the day that there simply wasn't enough money in the bank to see the thing through—and then, at half past the eleventh hour, having the best-paying magazine in the country buy one of my stories.

At last the final problems sank away and it was time to go, and I loaded everything into my old station wagon and drove the eight hundred miles from my apartment in Berkeley, California, to Flagstaff, Arizona, where I had some last-minute administrative details to tie down.

I do not think I ever really considered that things might go seriously wrong. I am still naïve enough to believe that if a man wants something badly enough he usually gets it. And I still wanted the Canyon. Wanted it badly.

Naturally, I had done all I could to keep it that way—to keep my dream fresh and untarnished, to shield it at all costs from familiarity, that sly and deadly anesthetic.

For one thing, I had decided after careful consideration that, except for some simple geology, I would do very little reading about the Canyon—no more than seemed necessary to extract vital information about routes and water sources. After all, I was not going down into the Canyon to learn intellectual facts.

I took similar precautions with the Canyon itself. On my first brief visit I had walked down a well-used tourist trail until I was several hundred feet below the Rim. What I saw had horrified and humbled and entranced me. It had been all the preview I needed; and I soon understood that it was also all I could allow. Later, in the planning stages, several people had said: "Why not fly over beforehand, low? That's the way to choose a safe route." But I had resisted the temptation.

When it came to siting the two food caches a delicate problem arose: I knew that if I packed stores down into the Canyon I would be "trespassing" in what I wanted to be unknown country; but I also knew that if I planted my caches outside the Rim I would in picking them up break both the real and symbolic continuity of my journey. In the end I solved the dilemma by siting each cache a few feet below the Rim.

Finally, when I had to hang around Grand Canyon Village for almost two weeks because of an infected heel, I went to the Rim no more than two or three times. Even then I took care to look only at the surface of what I saw.

And it worked. My dream survived.

Then, late one mid-April day, the dream faded quietly away and the reality was born.

Midway through his successful traverse of Grand Canyon National Park, Colin Fletcher began to realize his dream of understanding the meaning of geologic time.—ED.

We sat and talked—Jim Bailey and a park naturalist and I—beside the shallow limestone cave in which I had hidden my cache, and for an hour the world beyond the Rim was almost real. For behind everything they said I heard murmurs of a life hemmed in by authority and convention, by money-thrust, by conflicting loyalties, by today and tomorrow.

But when they went back up over the Rim they took the murmurs with them. And soon it was as if they had never sat with me beside the cave, and I moved back into my own world. I watched a tiny red spider scurry mad patterns on a stone. I ran my hand over the layered white walls of the limestone cave. I let myself ride with the cloud shadows, far below, across Darwin Plateau and up the white dome called Mount Huethawali and out over the dark Inner Gorge and then on and over the sun-baked rock terraces until at last we soared up and out and away beyond the distant white cliffs that were the North Rim.

In late afternoon I transferred into my canteens, very carefully, the water from the two-gallon-size wine bottles that formed part of the cache; and, because I had immediate plans for the five-gallon can that held the next week's supplies, I stuffed it, still unpacked, into my pack bag. In the cool of evening I started back down Bass Trail.

There was no hurry now. I had food for a week, and the trail led directly down to the river and the safety of unlimited water. I walked slowly, stopping when I wanted to. I stopped to look, unsuccessfully, for some ancient cliff dwellings the naturalist had mentioned. I stopped to look, also unsuccessfully, for cockleshells and other fossils in the white beds of limestone. And when I moved down out of limestone into sandstone—the same pale brown sandstone that had quietened me on the first evening of my journey, below Hualapai Hilltop—I stopped for a moment to consider with some surprise that ever since I climbed up onto the terrace above Supai, two weeks earlier, I had followed the same red layers of interleaved shale and sandstone that I had climbed up onto above Supai. On the two brief occasions I had left these layers—the reconnaissance of Fossil Canyon and the scramble up to Apache Point—there had been no time to stand and stare. But now it would be different. I had time to walk slowly, antennae spread, down through every layer of the Canyon's sculpture, from Rim to river.

A year before, at the Visitor Center, I had learned that each of these layers was a page in the earth's autobiography. And I had learned, intellectually, that the pages, taken together, revealed more of the earth's past than you can see from any other single place on its surface. I had, of course, moved down through these same layers on my way to the Inner Gorge reconnaissance. But at that time I had not been ready to read them: I was still jangling with the stubby rhythms of the world beyond the Rim.

I walked on down Bass Trail. It hairpinned through the brown sandstone, just as the trail had done below Hualapai Hilltop. And all at once I found myself standing in front of a little grotto. It was no more, really, than a hollow eroded back into the rock; a roofed-over shelf, ten feet long, four feet deep, and perhaps two feet high. But in the very center of its entrance, seeming to support the roof, stood a buttress. The buttress was, I knew, merely the chance result of erosion, a relic of rock that would in the slow and inexorable course of time dwindle beneath the wind and water that had carved it until at last it crumbled and vanished. But now, at this particular point in time, it was a beautiful thing.

The buttress merged with roof and floor in flowing and perfectly proportioned curves. And on its face was superimposed a small, delicately sculptured column, so oddly weathered that it seemed almost a decorative afterthought. The surface of this column was rounded and smooth, as if it had been sandpapered by a patient carpenter, and its fine-drawn strata stood out sharp and clear, like the grain on unstained, highly polished wood. The column's irregular outline flowed quite independently of the buttress's: it meandered upward, narrowed to a neck, then merged into a massive, curving superstructure of heavily bedded rockbands. And these bands, slanting down at a slight angle to the strata of both column and buttress, dominated the grotto and fused each element of it into a single harmony of curve and crosscut, grain and color, light and enigmatic shade.

For a long time I stood and looked at the grotto, feeling for something I knew was there but could not quite reach. At last I turned and walked on down the trail. But now, as I walked, I found myself looking at the rock more closely, thinking it more closely, feeling it more closely. It seemed as if all at once I could recognize, in some new and more thorough way—without any sense of revelation, just with an easy acceptance—how time, sandpapering rock, had created harmony and beauty. (But, after all, what was beauty but some kind of harmony between the rock and my senses?) And as I walked on down the trail I found that now at last I could comprehend the reality of what had happened to build the sandstone from which time had carved the grotto. I could comprehend it more than intellectually now, so that I could almost feel the dust stinging my bare legs. For the sandstone had been built by the same kind of wind and the same kind of dust that had blown at Hualpai Hilltop. The wind had whipped the dust along and then had dropped it, grain after grain, layer after layer, foot after foot—and had gone on doing so day after year after decade after century after millennium for perhaps ten million years, until at last it had built a layer of sand more than three hundred feet thick. Then the slow cementing action of water and colossal pressure had converted sand into rock. Into rock that preserved the outlines of rolling dunes as tilted strata. As strata that might stand out, where chance and time created a cliff face, as the crosscut grain on a decorative column or the slanting line of a massive rockband. A band that might, given the right random erosion, help fuse the harmonies of an exquisite little grotto. It was very simple, really. The only thing the wind and the dust needed was time.

And now I found that I was ready to grant them the time. For at last I could look, steadily, beyond today and tomorrow. And beyond yesterday, I could accept the day after century after millennium after millennium after slow millennium during which the wind had blown the dust in pale clouds across rolling sand dunes. I knew now how it had been. The dust had filled up a hollow here and a hollow there, built new dunes beside them, filled the new hollows—on and on and on, layer upon layer, until the sand lay three hundred feet thick. Then some slow, chance movement of the earth's crust happened to submerge the dunes beneath a shallow sea and tiny white-shelled creatures began their task of living and dying, living and dying, living and dying, until they had built above the sand the four-hundred-foot layer of limestone that now formed the Canyon's Rim. Yes, it was very simple, really. And now I could accept it all, without effort and as a part of my natural range of thought. As a part of my natural range of thought, that was the important thing.

I came down out of the sandstone onto familiar red rock and walked across Darwin Plateau. And as the light failed I camped close under the white dome of Mount Huethawali, quite near Huxley Terrace and only just around the corner from Evolution Amphitheater.

I camped, for nostalgia's sake, beside a big juniper tree. The juniper grew on the brink of the Redwall, and beyond it there opened up, as there had opened up on other evenings, a gray shape-filled pit. But this time, because I knew that in the morning I would go down into the pit, its shapes held new meaning. As darkness fell they seemed to challenge me; even, at first, to menace.

But in the morning it was different. There was an interval of superb synchronization when, at exactly the moment the moon sank behind the Rim and the pit's blue-black shadows eased over into black, a paleness began to invade the eastern sky. The shadows faded. Vague shapes crystallized, as they always did, into butte and cliff and mesa. Soon daylight had filled the pit with its colossal, solid sculpture. But when, after breakfast, I walked on down Bass Trail—acutely aware once more of the pages of the earth's autobiography—I no longer looked at the sculpture. Instead, my eyes sought out the strata that gave the sculpture meaning.

Below my nightcamp the trail swung around to the right and angled down across the face of the Redwall in a man-made cutting. Here the story of the earth was no longer written in grains of sand. The smooth red rock under my feet had been built—much as the white upper limestone had been built—by the shells of minute organisms that had lived and died by the millions upon millions in an ancient sea and had gone on living and dying and sinking to the sea bed until their corpses had built a layer of blue-gray rock six hundred feet deep. A rock whose surface has been stained red by water seeping down from the red, iron-bearing strata above. Yes, it was all very simple still, and very easy to accept.

I moved down deeper into the Canyon.

Soon I was walking over interleaved layers, purple and green, of shale that had once been mud swirling down an ancient river that flowed long before the Colorado existed. Mud that had come to rest at last, thick and soft, off some primordial shore. Had come to rest in the same way that thick, soft mud is coming to rest today off the mouth of the Colorado and forming mud flats that will probably, in due time, become new layers of shale or slate.

I moved down yet deeper.

On the brink of the Inner Gorge I passed through a band of dark brown sandstone. (This time, it was sand from a beach.) And then, below the sandstone, I stepped down into a different world.

All at once, black and twisted rocks pressed in on me—rocks that had been so altered by time and heat and pressure that no one can tell for sure what their original form was. And as I walked down between them, sinking deeper into a narrow cleft that forms one of the rare major breaks in the wall of the Inner Gorge, I felt again, as I had not felt since my reconnaissance, the oppression of insignificance.

I walked on down. The cleft deepened. The black rock pressed closer, almost shutting out the sky. And then, quite suddenly, I had stepped out onto a broad rock platform. A hundred feet below me the river was sparkling blue-green and white. And the sky had opened up again.

I sat and rested on the rock platform, looking over and beyond the river at the strata on strata that mounted one on the other to the North Rim. I could see them all, every layer. They were replicas of those I had just moved down through. And after I had sat and looked at them for a while I saw that now, from a distance, I could see with eye and intellect what I had all day been understanding through instinct. Now, as my eye traveled downward from the Rim, it watched the rocks grow older.

It watched them grow older in a way that would have been impossible when I was living, day after day, surrounded and cushioned and segregated by the accouterments of the man-ruled world—by chairs and electricity and money-thrust and the rest of the tinsel. I knew that when I returned to that world I would probably remember what I saw as a flight of fancy, as airy symbolism. But at the time, as I sat there on the rock platform above the sparkling river, the pageant I saw spread out before me shone with a reality as rich as any I have ever caught in the beam of logic.

I saw, when I looked up at the Rim, that the uppermost layers of rock were bright and bold and youthful. Their unseamed faces shone pink or white or suntan-brown, untouched by the upheavals that time brings to all of us. But below the Redwall they began to show their age. There, in staid maturity, they wore dark greens and subdued browns. And their faces had begun to wrinkle. Then, as my eye reached the lip of the Inner Gorge, the rocks plunged into old age. Now they wore gray and sober black. The wrinkles had deepened. And their features had twisted beneath the terrible weight of the years. Old age had come to them, just as it comes in the end to all of us who live long enough.

I rested on the rock platform for an hour. Then I clambered down to the river through the darkest and most twisted rock of all. Once more, as on the Inner Gorge reconnaissance, every boulder and hanging fragment of the rock around me looked ready to come crashing down at any minute. But now I needed no tight and determined thinking to ward off fear. During my three weeks among crumbling rockfaces and loose talus, all apparently waiting to crash headlong at any minute, I had heard just once—a long way off—the sound of a small stone falling a very short distance. And now I understood why.

The poised boulders and fragments were indeed waiting to crash down at any minute. But there was not really too much danger that one would hit me during that particular hiccup of time we humans called May 1963. For our human clocks and the geologic clock kept different times. "Any minute now," geologic time, meant only that several fragments of rock might fall before May 2063, and that quite an appreciable number would probably do so by May 11963. I knew this now, through and through. I might not yet understand the explicit, absolute meaning of two hundred million years. But I had come to grips with the kind of geology I had hoped to find. I had begun at last to hear the rhythm of the rock.

I have heard rumors of visitors who were disappointed. The same people will be disappointed at the Day of Judgment. In fact, the Grand Canyon is a sort of landscape Day of Judgment. It is not a showplace, a beauty spot, but a revelation. . . . It is the world's supreme example of erosion. But this is not what it really is. It is, I repeat, a revelation. The Colorado River made it, but you feel when you are there that God gave the Colorado River its instruction. . . . Even to remember that it is there lifts up the heart. J. B. PRIESTLEY

THE BOATMAN'S CANYON

Between the time of John Wesley Powell's first recorded descent of the Colorado River through Grand Canyon in 1869 and the Second World War, only about one hundred people accepted the challenge of one of the world's wildest stretches of white water. But the advent of more suitable boats, particularly the inflatable neoprene raft with its amazing buoyancy and flexibility, greatly expanded the coterie of river runners. Professional guides began to conduct regularly scheduled trips through the Canyon safe enough for women and children. Now as many as a thousand make the run in a single summer month, and the trend is upward. The impact of this relatively heavy recreational use of the fragile wilderness in the Canyon's bottom has become a source of concern to the National Park Service. Still the Canyon voyage is a rare adventure in one of the last, really vast wildernesses in continental United States. No road crosses or parallels the Colorado River from Navajo Bridge across Marble Gorge to Hoover Dam, a distance of 350 river miles. And the Colorado's major rapids are close to the limits of navigability, even with improved boats. So one still leaves Lee's Ferry, Arizona, the jumping-off place, with an involuntary tightening of the throat.

*Three men who ran the river in the recent past here share their impressions. Ernest Braun's journal demonstrates that great photographs are the result of a man's reacting as well as a film's. For Stewart L. Udall, Secretary of the Interior when he ran the Colorado, the trip was both business and pleasure. Mr. Udall was in the midst of making a judgment about the proposed Grand Canyon dams. Braun's log and my own were written in large part "on the spot" and often by flashlight or firelight. These three accounts, and the photographs all through this book, suggest what the men who wrote and took them know—that the Grand Canyon's greatest challenge is internal. Can a man respond in full measure to the universe of beauty and inspiration spread before him? On the river one dares one's own unknown as well as the Canyon's.—*ED.

It is difficult to conceive of a region uninhabited by man. We habitually presume his presence and influence everywhere. And yet we have not seen pure Nature unless we have seen her thus vast and drear and inhuman. . . . Nature was here something savage and awful, though beautiful. . . . This was that Earth of which we have heard, made out of Chaos and Old Night. Here was no man's garden, but the unhanseled globe. . . . Man was not to be associated with it. It was Matter, vast, terrific. . . . There was clearly felt the presence of a force not bound to be kind to man. It was a place for heathenism and superstitious rites,—to be inhabited by men nearer of kin to the rocks and to wild animals than we.

HENRY DAVID THOREAU

The river is the most complete host for a visit to the Grand Canyon.

It will carry our boats for us, keep our supplies cool and moist,
amuse us and sometimes excite us as it glides us into a walled-in world

where layer after layer of old rock rises up
until the great Redwall limestone dominates Marble Gorge.

The river feeds the gardens that nourish the myriad insects,
all providing for the birds and animals, freely moving,
yet dependent on the river shore to live.

The streams, here lucid, there turbid, support
tiny collections of living things, each carrying out its errand,
in a small world where water, rock, plant, and animal continually work out
ways of getting along as part of the universe of the Grand Canyon.

The change of natural things still succeeds, here subtly . . . .

. . . . *there dramatically.*

*We can succeed here too, as visitors, delighting in the aromas
we can coax from a stove and fire of our own making.*

We can let the living river succeed with us, feel its grip,
and hear river music with no whining motor to drown it out.

We can go ashore, feel its texture underfoot—
and sometimes take our footprints with us.

We can be awed by the enormity of what looked small
only because the Canyon can dwarf everything within it.

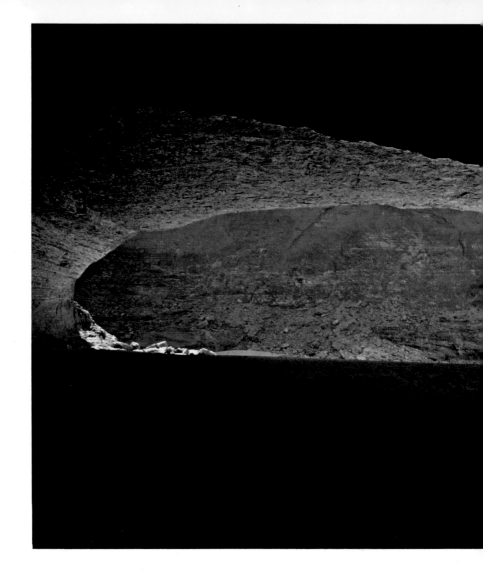

Redwall Cavern, the largest cave open to view
in the Canyon wall and reached from the river,
could seat fifty thousand people.
But let Redwall Cavern be found in quiet; let it be lonely

Spirit that form'd this scene,
These tumbled rock-piles grim and red,
These reckless, heaven-ambitious peaks,
These gorges, turbulent-clear streams,
        this naked freshness,
These formless wild arrays,
        for reasons of their own,
I know thee, savage spirit—
        we have communed together.

WALT WHITMAN

Rapids happen because of big rocks and little, young, old,
and incredibly ancient, down from Hermit, and Hance, from Badger,
from Tapeats and Kanab and Stone Creek, and Shinumo and Coconino.
They assemble in order, gather together, so the Colorado can sand them down
and take them away, in the natural, relentless levelling of the land.

Rapids have a spirit of their own, good to commune with
if there is a boatman along who knows that
the river can be fun, but isn't to be trifled with.

Your knuckles may get white, but after the first rapid or two they relax.

Then a good thing can happen. The spirit of the rapid and your spirit become one. You exult as your boat dashes on it, turning, climbing, plowing, powered by the river and guided by a nimble oar, rampaging on to the end, where in whirlpools and surges the river finds its pieces and pulls them together again.

What use are rapids?
What use are we if we remain indifferent to challenge?
What are we worth if we won't feel exhilaration?

*Side streams that bring the rock down reveal the story of the canyon
as only a side stream can, attenuating the strata that the river cuts so sharply.*

*Row hard at the last minute and you can beach your boat
where the muddy Colorado receives the crystal waters of Tapeats Creek.*

*Climb a little, and Tapeats will guide you
to its best-known, best-hidden tributary, Thunder River.*

We can watch Thunder foam out into the light, giving no hint
of its dark beginnings under the high Kaibab Plateau,
where snow fell and melted, and rain trickled into limestone.
In black narrow vaults the waters convene and tumble out in cascades
to water one of the finest gardens in Grand Canyon.

Like Cedric Wright, "We are aware, lying under trees,
of the roots and directions of our whole being.
Perceptions drift in from earth and sky. A vast healing begins."

Elves' Chasm is easy to reach from the river.
It hides its falls and pools. There are more and more for those who look.

The truth Loren Eiseley wrote becomes clear:
"If there is magic on this planet, it is contained in water."

Like Thunder Creek, Deer Creek is not in the national park. It ought to be.

Havasu is protected in the national park—as long as the park is protected.
The way we come in is tight and winding where
the creek has worn down through.
Or take the trail from the rim and be drawn down
by the beauty the stream promises and constantly creates,
good to look upon and equally good to feel.

And there are more and more side canyons, too many for a lifetime,
but not too many for the lifetimes of those who will find their way here,
to discover what Thoreau believed would always be awaiting man,
"a world visibly recreated in the night."

To explore, to be within and part of the wildness of this place,
to begin to learn what it can tell, confirms the idea
that some land should be left unimpaired,
that all people might come and enjoy it for what it is—
the national park idea.

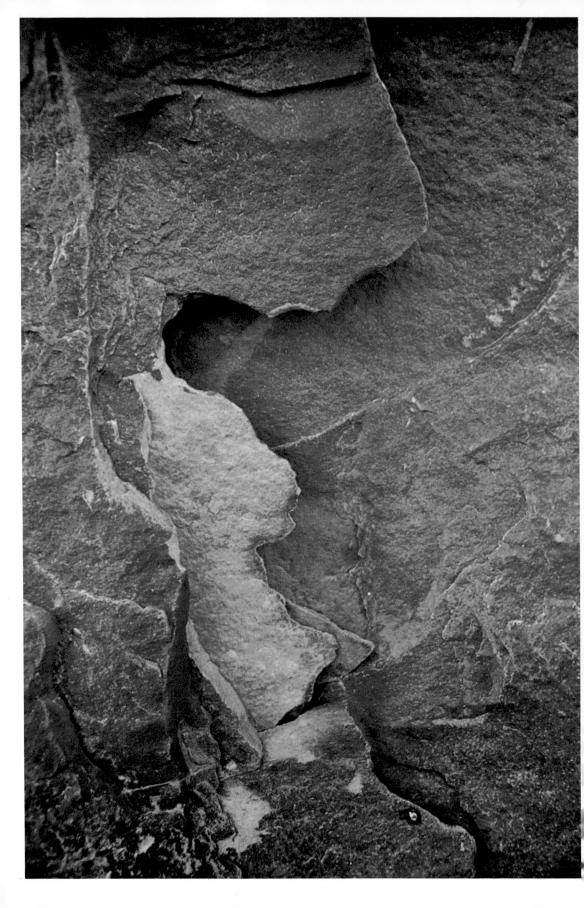

Colorado River Journal

ERNEST BRAUN

WHEN MY FRIEND Clyde Childress invited me to go through the Grand Canyon on a river trip, I had just returned from a two-week knapsack trip into the southern Sierra, and it seemed like time to go back to work. My family, however, knowing how much the trip would mean to me, insisted that I go. Our boats, three belonging to Martin Litton and one to Clyde Childress, averaged sixteen feet in length and carried a party of thirteen.

SEPTEMBER 12

Lee's Ferry was the starting point of our river trip. We got up at 5:30, finished packing the boats, and we finally pushed off about 10 A.M.

We moved off serenely with the current, which is gentle here. The Grand Canyon starts officially, from a geologic point of view, a few hundred yards below Lee's Ferry where the Kaibab limestone appears. As we moved downriver, the canyon walls got higher, and more formations appeared with their different colors and textures.

This first day was loaded with so many impressions that it would take all of it to write them down—there is so much to take in: the river itself, its surface always changed by the current, the wind, the sun, and best of all, the reflections from the cliffs, and the panorama of rock walls as we glide by at about the speed of a fast walk; my eyes never stop. At water level, there are caves and glistening erosion marks, and the brilliant green tamarisk with flowers, white to purple, line the banks in some places. Looking up, you see towers, arches, and needles along the canyon rim. Colors are everywhere, from white to brilliant red. The river is fairly clear here, its sediment settled out in Lake Powell, just upstream.

We ran two rapids today—Badger and Soap Creek. The procedure is to land all the boats at the head of the rapid. (My job is to jump out and tie up to a secure rock.) Then the boatmen climb down the shore, and decide where and how to run their boats. Often Martin goes first while the other boatmen watch. If he is right, and he usually is, they go the same way. If he is wrong, they try not to make the same mistake. I have learned to always jump out with a camera or two, and shoot his boat before we go through.

The ride is like a roller coaster. Sometimes we come through dry, and sometimes we are completely soaked and have much bailing to do. It will take a lot of practice to click the shutter at the right time for I tend to duck instead of shoot when a wave rolls over us. We camped just below Soap Creek.

SEPTEMBER 13

I got up early and re-organized my camera gear so that I have more tools at hand to work with and so I can quickly take my gear with me when we stop. I really started to work today. Our lunch stop was on a small beach under a large overhanging shelf. I got a good close-up of animal tracks unidentified in the mud.

Our adventure today was that our boatman, François Leydet, fell out as we pitched high and sideways in the rapids. He hung onto the boat and I pulled him back in. It happened so fast that I couldn't decide whether to grab the oars myself, keep taking pictures, or jump in to pull him back to the boat. We came through okay, and I got one picture of him in the water before I pulled him in.

SEPTEMBER 14

I am writing a day late, even though it is hard to remember the day before; there wasn't time from dawn to dusk, but tonight there is enough wood to have a bonfire to write by. Wood will be diminishing from now on, as no more washes down the river because of Glen Canyon Dam. We were off by 8:30 A.M. Early morning and late afternoon are best for taking pictures on the river—there are more reflections and variation in light. Everything glows when the sun hits one wall of the canyon and bounces into the shadowed river.

About 11 A.M., our boat hit a rock in the rapids. We felt a solid thump but thought no damage was done. Almost immediately afterward François told me to sit down, as the boat was unbalanced. I checked the compartment on that side, and it was full of water. We bailed like mad until we came to a place we could beach the boat. We all pulled it onto the beach and water poured out of a hole right near where the side and the bottom came together. We had a 3-hour delay while the hole was patched.

Each beach we camp on is different and seems more beautiful in its own way, but so far we have spent so much time pulling boats out of the river, packing and unpacking, that it cuts down on picture-taking time. My duffle bag was in the flooded compartment and everything was wet except my clothes in a waterproof box. This included my two boxes of tobacco, matches, kleenex, and first aid kit. I spread out the tobacco on a shirt, and it dried out okay. I thought of John Wesley Powell spreading out his flour to dry.

Our camp is near the mouth of a canyon, but we have no time to explore it. I always find many new and exciting shrubs and grasses growing in the sand. Of course, there is no need to get a picture of everything, but the visual scene is all new and fresh to me and infinitely exciting.

SEPTEMBER 15

We had easy sailing today, with no mistakes. At mid-morning we pulled in and climbed to Stanton's Cave, about 150 feet above the river in the limestone formations we are going through. It is one of hundreds we have passed. We explored a series of caverns and found three bent twig figurines made by Indians more than 4,000 years ago. This cave has been extensively studied, so what we found must have been imperfect pieces that were discarded. The figurines are no more than three inches long and are mostly in the shape of deer.

We had lunch in the Redwall Cavern on a beach under a massive, arch-shaped overhang. We passed the site of Marble Canyon Dam this afternoon. There was nothing to see except a steel scaffold about 100 feet high on each bank. As we landed to look, I sunk into mud up to my shorts. A most inhospitable spot.

SEPTEMBER 16

This evening, as I write, I am using my flashlight, so I will make it short. This morning early, I walked up Spook Canyon and photographed the first spring, which is surrounded by maidenhair fern, with the red wall of the canyon across the river in the background.

I saw and photographed a deer and her fawn running along the river. I have seen a blue heron, some ducks, bats, and other small birds. Tonight François found a canyon rattlesnake near where he and I are sleeping, and I got some good pictures for my son. This rattler is the color of the rocks, a dusty pinkish brown with faint markings. Evidently, it is quite rare, so we are fortunate.

We made 25 miles today, with few stops, for most of the rapids were small. I switched boats and I plan to try all the boats for the best picture platform. The time passes very fast on the river. The rapids are really not very scary. Roaring as they do, they sound worse than they are. And you could walk around most of them if you wanted. The stars are as clear as in the Sierra, but I have not been awake long enough to enjoy them fully. I am going to have to discipline myself to shoot more Kodachrome; the high speed Ektachrome is going too fast.

SEPTEMBER 17

Our boat ride today was short. We landed at noon after sailing down a canyon that was still very volcanic and open. At our last camp we found some pieces of old pottery 700 to 1,000 years old. We are camping just above Hance Rapid, which is supposed to be one of the two worst on the river. Martin has not decided whether to run it or line it, but we will wait until morning, as the river level is bad right now.

Rapids are very beautiful, especially from above. They start with a tongue of smooth oily water that breaks up into waves. Almost always you go down the middle of the tongue, or a little to one side in the main flow. Often the boatman goes sideways down the tongue and at the last second turns the boat into the first wave, and then tries to hit the wave head-on and avoid the deepest holes between the waves as well as any rocks that may be around. At the edge of the rapid are eddies and whirlpools that sometimes move upstream. The boatman tries to keep out of these, for he loses time and control. When waves are too high or close to each other, the boat does not have time to come up for each one; then it is very wet in the boat. When waves come from different angles, perhaps bouncing off the canyon walls, it is hard to run them at the right angle. If these erratic waves are big and the boatman loses control, the boat may flip over.

Right after lunch I set out for our first hike. We had a choice of trails. Instead of going up Red Canyon, we took the Tonto trail that parallels the river about 500 feet above it. It was good to put on hiking boots again. Naturally, the river looks very different from above. We found lovely cactus and gorgeous rocks.

We ate a lazy dinner around the fire and had a good sleep. Hiking today I realized how warm it is. We took along a gallon canteen, and the three of us drank it in about six miles.

There are sand dunes near our camp just loaded with animal tracks, and at dusk they make great pictures. I got one that looks like a freeway for snakes, birds, mice, lizards and deer. I am constantly amazed at how bright the green things are along the river. The pictures will look unnatural.

SEPTEMBER 18

Martin has decided to line one boat through Hance first to pick up people on the other boats that might get into trouble. This is hard and dangerous work, especially today for the river has turned the color of hot chocolate with a load of mud. You cannot see where your feet are going, and when you wade into the current, with the lines holding the boat, you slip and slide over boulders and rocks. My pictures should be very good of this operation.

Martin ran through first and we could hear him, above the water noise, thump against two rocks, but there was no damage.

We ran two more huge rapids today—Sockdologer and Grapevine—with the biggest waves yet. Several boats hit rocks, and one needed repair on a tiny beach.

Here in the Granite Gorge the walls come right down into the water. We are going through the Vishnu schist formation, which is just gorgeous. It's almost black, and it has an iridescent glow where polished by the water. The black is broken up by a pink granite and thin dikes or stripes of white quartz.

I got a surprise dunking, and a good laugh for everybody but me, while jumping onto this polished granite to tie up the boat. I stepped over to what I thought was a mud bank and went into where my hat did not even show. Unfortunately I had an exposure meter in my pocket—ruined.

It was a busy afternoon bailing all the time and shooting the rest of the time. Cameras and everything else are now muddy, as there is no way to clean anything. I have it rigged now so I have three cameras and my waterproof Nikonos in the waterproof cans beside me. I have to keep constantly alert that the cans are shut tight when the going is wet and rough.

In the back of my mind I am also figuring ways of interpreting all this visually. I feel there is much more to be done, and I am unsatisfied with my efforts. On the river there is no time to plan; everything changes so quickly.

SEPTEMBER 19

We slept at Phantom Ranch, the only buildings in Grand Canyon, and it was strange to wake up in a bed this morning, with the rain coming down hard. I had my worst night's sleep of the trip. I had the feeling that I needed a vacation from the canyon today. It is so overpowering that I seem to be concentrating all the time. I felt lazy and took my time getting down to the boats. On the way I had to stop and shoot raindrops on the mesquite. I rearranged and repacked my gear.

We had two wild rides today—Horn and Granite Falls, with the biggest waves yet. I went out photographing after making camp, and went out of my mind for a while trying to catch the subtle color and shapes here. Rocks I never knew existed, and all over bullrushes, all along the stream, add a new element. I always have to work fast; the light goes quickly in the canyon.

Where the clear water of the creek meets the muddy Colorado I shot the beautiful, delicate patterns of the mixing waters.

This is such a good Earth when you see it laid bare for thousands of feet in the canyon. Its skin and bones, exposed as they are, make glorious feelings in me as I gaze around in astonishment.

SEPTEMBER 20

Martin and I went down Hermit Rapid first and got a good morning shower on the way. I photographed the other boats coming through. They are the best rapid pictures yet, as the waves were huge with big holes between, and with good backlight on the muddy water.

SEPTEMBER 21

We started again with a morning shower through the first rapid and stopped before lunch at Elves' Chasm—a narrow canyon rising steeply from the beach, with a waterhole and fern gardens. Dave Brower, Jeff, and Bob went ahead. I tried climbing above the first falls by myself. Clyde warned me away from some bad spots, but I scared myself crawling on ledges that went nowhere. Finally, I made it by leaving some of my camera gear behind me.

At lunch on the beach below, Dave described their climb, which was far beyond and up. He said they had found the most beautiful spot he had ever seen. I mentioned that I wished I had gone with them, so after lunch he offered to take me back up, with any others who wanted to go. I threw a camera into an ammo can attached to a line, for we had to climb through the falls up above. I was sure I would not make it after Dave fell on one of the steep parts back into the pool below, but I did, along with Jeff, Bob, Clyde, Ty, Hugh, and Dobie. I found that the answer is to rock climb with experienced people who know what they are doing. The climb was a thrill, and Dave was right—at the top of the canyon was a fern and moss garden with exquisite detail, and the wall of the canyon on the other side of the river was reflected in the pools. All the ferns were maidenhair, with flowers that were new to me. The whole river trip was worth it, only for these three hours. Dave is very quiet, but he seems to have great appreciation for beauty, and also a very stubborn set to his chin.

The canyon is wide, and we can occasionally see the rim. We looked all day for mountain sheep, and I had my 300mm lens ready, but no luck. Today, I did what I have always wanted on a river trip—explore along the way.

As I write by flashlight, which is not good, the moon is shining on the upper walls of the canyon. We will have more of it every night. I hope to take some moonlight pictures.

I am writing again by flashlight. We are back in Vishnu schist and Tapeats sandstone. This dark granite gleams like metal in the sun. We ran only two big rapids this morning. In Bedrock, which has a sharp bend, the trick is to make the bend and not hit the rock at the turn. All went well. We had lunch at Stone Creek with good fresh water and a natural shower. This side canyon goes into the north bank of the canyon and gets more sun than Elves' Canyon. The lush, almost tropical growth of grasses and reeds and horsetail reminds me of Hawaii. Farther up grow cottonwoods that are beautiful against the purple canyon across the river. The rim is 5,000 feet above us here. We see it occasionally and can count the formations we have come through.

Everyone seems to be feeling better today. Tomorrow we will spend all day hiking up Tapeats Creek to Thunder River, and we will explore another cave. It is possible to backpack down Tapeats Canyon from the rim and to walk along the river to Deer Creek. This is something to think about—maybe next Easter vacation. It was beautiful on the river at dusk.

SEPTEMBER 23

I just got out of a cold water bath by moonlight in Tapeats Creek, which is cold, clear, and fast running, with lots of trout to be caught. I sit here on my sleeping bag in the sand relishing this day, which has been great indeed.

At about 8 A.M. we left camp on Tapeats Creek, which flows at first between steep vertical cliffs. To start with, you have to climb around up a talus slope and skirt the cliff tops, coming down to the stream in a half mile or so. We followed it about three miles, crossing every so often through cottonwoods, cactus, mesquite, and catclaw. It is just like Budd Creek, except that the walls around us are layered with yellow, brown, and red, and there are great vistas of the canyon up to the rim in the distance. The light today was superb—lots of clouds and occasional thunder and showers. It is one of the truly great hikes of my life. I am sure that pictures cannot say it.

After innumerable picture stops we reached the foot of Thunder River, which comes into Tapeats Creek from the left, down a canyon about 1,000 feet high and a mile long, with intermittent cascades and waterfalls below the opening in the rock where Thunder River comes out of the canyon wall. It is really just a huge spring. All along it are trees, ferns, and flowers. The contrast of this green and white water ribbon on the bare canyon wall is quite unbelievable.

You can climb up to and into the two caves where the water comes out, but the last hundred feet are very steep and require all arms, hands, and legs. There is a ledge that stops at a corner, and you have to step across open space and around the corner. This stopped some of our gang and was really pretty scary without a rope, but not hard to do. Then up a few almost vertical feet, with hand and foot holds, to the entrance of the cave, with all that water gushing through just under you as you inch in, by friction of hands, feet, and back. Everything about it was glorious, but as I went back down the trail by myself, I thought that while beautiful, this is hostile country to be alone in. Days like this are rare in a lifetime. We will have to come back.

September 24

It was a full, varied, and exciting day again. I'm writing by candlelight. Our boat spilled in a little rapid called Fishtail. A wave hit us at the wrong angle and we were in the water with the boat on top of us the next thing we knew. All I remember is kicking loose a rope around my leg, and then bobbing along beside the boat. I had had my pipe in my mouth all the time and did not realize it until we beached the boat to right it a few minutes later. One of my ammo cases containing a couple of cameras had broken loose, but it floated and someone snagged it for me. All we lost were our hats and couple of bailing buckets.

We hiked into Deer Creek today before lunch. Each canyon has a quality of its own. At Deer Creek the falls come right out of the Canyon wall close to the river. To get back into it, we climbed the talus and cliff about 200 feet and walked back along a ledge a few hundred yards long that looks down into a very narrow, deep canyon where Deer Creek flows. It opens out finally into a small valley with trees. After some fooling around and misgivings, I was able to climb down to the stream bed and walk back toward the river quite a way. My best shots were down behind one of the little waterfalls.

After lunch, we went on down the river to Kanab Creek—wide, deep, and massive. There are gorgeous light reflections in the water, and mud riffles and dried, cracked red clay along the sides. I thought this was one of the most beautiful places we had seen: I could have worked there for days instead of an hour.

We had to leave and continue downstream, where we are camped in a narrow gorge that reminds me of the upper river. It is possible to hike all the way up Kanab Creek to the rim. Again, it's a good backpacking possibility.

September 25

This day was notable for many things, mostly wildlife. We saw our first bighorn sheep, which are about the color of deer. I did not get any pictures, however. Then we saw an ibis and I got a good picture of a big lizard called a chuckwalla.

Then tonight in camp at Fern Glen we saw another rattler. All I had loaded was Kodachrome, so I made some half-second exposures—one when he was moving. It may be beautiful.

The only major rapid was Upset, which upset no one. I got a couple of slow motion shots. I am going to try more of them from now on.

Our big treat was Havasu Creek, where we spent about three hours. We took the boats up it for a short distance, pushing by hand along the sides. The boat having the broadest beam just made it through when we all stood on one side to tilt it a little. This was fun, but the beautiful part is following the creek up the canyon. There are many little waterfalls and a sort of dwarf horsetail all along the water. Grass that looked like Bermuda grass, but more lush, and a vine that must have been some variety of grape grow there as well as ocotilla. Havasu has a very pretty, fairyland quality. It could be the garden of Eden.

We are going through one of the most beautiful parts of the Grand Canyon. It's very grand with towering red cliffs, just as one might suppose it should look, and the river is muddy.

In spite of my constant search for the one picture that will really say it, I kind of took the afternoon off. I had used up all my fast film and did not dig into the hatch to get my bag that has my supply. And because François insisted on going first I had no boat ahead of me when the light was right, so I relaxed and dozed. We found a little brandy. We sang and had water fights and were silly. It really felt like a Sunday afternoon.

We will have time to explore Fern Glen in the morning, and then we hit Lava Falls, the terror of the river. It's getting late—all of 8:00 P.M.—so lights out.

SEPTEMBER 26

We spent a leisurely morning for a change. I feel fine after last night's sleep.

Our rattler from last night came down to drink in the river during the night and left some beautiful tracks, which I just photographed, right between our sleeping bags. It just shows that we are all good neighbors.

Fern Glen is dry this time and, while beautiful, is not as photogenic as the other canyons. The fern banks get a little seepage but badly need a good rain, which may come tonight according to my figuring.

It is very overcast now. We came 11 miles today and are camped above the dreaded Lava Falls. We did not run it tonight; the water is low.

The canyon has opened out and there are lava formations, very hard, like basalt. This makes Lava Falls rough, for the top of the rapid is literally a waterfall over hard lava rock, and there are other rocks in it. I would like to run it in one of the boats and face the boatman to photograph his expressions, and then shoot the other boats from the shore. I am glad we stopped here because I got shots of some limestone springs near the campsite.

Tonight, we had watercress for salad which we found by one of the springs. Delightful.

SEPTEMBER 27

Just as I start to write, the sprinkles begin again, but not for long, I hope. This morning was very overcast. Everybody got up early with various kinds of anticipation for Lava Falls. Martin finally went first. Okay. Then François. Okay. After taking pictures of them I was third, with John.

I put my pipe and spoon into an ammunition case, I wound the Nikonos strap tightly around my wrist, and we were off. I sat on top of the back compartment, bracing my knees on the seat below and holding onto the ends of the two extra oars on either side of me, which I thought were very secure. I planned to hang on through the first big drop and then start shooting. We went over and down, and the oars I was holding came loose from the turbulence and shock—and so did I, right over the side. So I went through Lava hanging to the emergency rope that is fastened along the side. It took all I had to hang on with both hands, going through the waves. I got no pictures, but I did not lose the camera. The boat filled, but I got in at the bottom, and that was that.

I got back into position with my camera for the last boat's run. From where I was, low and near the water, it just disappeared. When the boat came up only the bottom showed with nobody hanging on. I spotted one of its occupants swimming for shore, and another finally showed downstream, but Clyde did not appear. In a minute or two—it seemed longer—I saw him climb onto a rock not far from where the boat spilled. It turned out to be a near tragedy: trying to rescue his camera he got out of the main current and was trapped in a rock tunnel under water. He tried to force his way upstream and out of the tunnel, but the force of the torrent imprisoned him. Finally, and fortunately, he relaxed, washed through, and popped out. Other than a few cuts and bruises, he is fine. I broke out the last of the beer—we needed it.

There's no time to be scared when you are in the rapid; you're too busy hanging on and getting air between waves.

Really, it was an exciting morning. Actually, very few wooden boats have been through Lava. Two made it last year and our four this time. Usually, they are lined or carried. It is less work and more fun our way.

We made 20 miles today, after Lava Falls all smooth, through fantastic lava columnar formations. It has been cloudy and cold with a good breeze blowing. We are just about at the 200-mile mark.

SEPTEMBER 28

Today it was clear, warm, relatively uneventful, and we had a very pleasant and relaxing run of 17 miles. A good current and few rapids made it a leisurely journey—with open canyon most of the way. It looks drier along the slopes, and there are many more varieties of cactus. We saw and photographed wild donkeys, and we saw a bobcat—though we only glimpsed his rear end as he ran, so we got no pictures. We had lunch under a large willow along the bank, and walked a mile or so up a dry wash.

We were going to camp at Three Springs Canyon, but its entrance is in the middle of a rapid and we could not get in, so we are camped a little below it. Some of us walked up along the canyon rim, which is low here, and brought back clear water.

Every night of the trip it has been warm enough to sit around only in shorts after dark, and we have always slept on clean sandy beaches and always have had plenty of wood. The sand is very white and fine all along the river.

I am pretty loose now, as most of my film is exposed, and I have made my statement and also my mistakes, and anything I get now will not add too much to it. I have been trying in the last few days to relate people to all the beautiful things I photograph; I know that some of this is important for scale and will make the rest more publishable. A picture from a boat is hard to get because you have to take it as it comes and the boats are never still—they constantly turn wih the current and eddies.

I have been worried about the built-in meter in the camera. I use it a lot, so I must keep checking on it. All I can do now is hope it has been right, because grabshots taken on the river are only possible with it. It is most important to have a camera around all the time in a situation like this; the most subtle things are very fleeting. They are seen and gone a moment later, and too often missed. I find that I am cherishing the beauty all around me, and the easy pace, and I almost cringe at the thought of going back into the world of freeways, telephones, and politics.

At this moment, before turning in, I see before me the canyon bright with moonlight, with the river softly moving at my feet. Earlier, we heard donkeys braying, and now there are only crickets, and rapids upstream grumbling steadily.

SEPTEMBER 29

This is our last night on the river. We passed Separation Canyon, Mile 240, and are at about Mile 245, making almost thirty miles today.

What a surprise this day has been. I had expected nothing, but the canyon narrowed, and we went through our most beautiful formations—brown, black, and pink granite, sculptured up to the high water level by the river into the most beautiful shapes I have seen. Also, there were lots of rapids—not bad enough to stop and look at, but with plenty of zing for a good wet ride. I hope I got the pictures I have been trying for, of the boatman's face and the waves around him.

We stopped at Travertine Springs and Travertine Falls, where water flowing through limestone is actually building rock as it redeposits the lime. Travertine Falls has a complete limestone structure that can be seen from the river where water-deposited rock, about 125 feet high, has assumed the shape of the falls.

We also passed the site of Hualapai Dam, which would back up water 94 miles to Kanab Creek and bury all the things we have seen below it. This just seems inconceivable after a day like today. The damsite is at about mile 237. Just below the damsite, we passed a wrecked boat that must have come up from Lake Mead and got fouled up in the first rapid. We have passed the last rapid, and now the river is not making a sound and is becoming wide and sluggish.

SEPTEMBER 30

It's up early in the morning to start rowing again, in case our pickup boats cannot get over the mud bar at the bank of the river.

Our tow boat met us between 10:00 and 11:00 A.M.

The second motorboat had engine trouble coming up and needed to be towed also when we reached it. Progress was slow for the towboat got stuck in a whole series of mud bars; then the whole row of boats would get snarled up. The water is so muddy it was hard to see the shallow places. Thus, erratically, we moved down Lake Mead to the Temple Bar roadhead and take-out point.

The banks of the lower stretch are all silted in, and none of the Canyon rock is visible. It's just like going between two earthen dikes. The exhaust fumes from the motor ahead were most unpleasant and added to the feeling of being a captive, after our days of freedom on the unfettered river.

EPILOGUE

Back in civilization I had a chance to muse over the dichotomy of the natural world and the world of man. The difference, besides the obvious physical environment, is one of feeling. I was still tuned to the wilderness wavelength for two or three days. After photographing, supposedly creatively, in a fruit and vegetable cannery for two days, I am all tensed up. The speed, the noise, and the fearsome, complicated, and spirit-dulling environment of a modern factory have brought me slowly back to human reality. One and a half million bottles of catsup a day, three million cans of tomatoes on a moving belt, eight hours a day. I felt uninspired, even with the freedom to photograph anything in the cannery. I just pushed myself through the day.

The feeling of wilderness only comes when you leave it; until then, if you can let yourself, you are to a degree part of it. What gets to you, unconsciously maybe, is that there is a long-time order and balance in wild country; that man is only a flash in the pan. The land and life of all the kingdoms, families and species live there independently and yet totally interdependently. Life in the wilderness goes on with such grand style and poise. Living in it we must adjust; our day is the sun's day. Of course we have the comfort and security of plentiful body nourishment for our time there, so we are not as involved as the wild burro looking for grass or the rattlesnake looking for dinner at dusk at our campsite. But we also have the contrast of man's world to compare with what we see and feel.

This feel of the natural world is the reward and the real and urgent reason for leaving wilderness around us. Without it, man cannot physically exist, but just as important, he will in time drive himself mad. Man has everything he needs to reshape the natural world for his immediate profit. Will he do it and thereby destroy the meaning of all life?

I am pessimistic about the sale and use of my wilderness pictures, especially after looking through the current flock of magazines—an almost total involvement with man's narrow little world, plus some interest in exploiting what is left, is their universal theme.

The world of man is lovely and great to be a part of in many ways, but without the perspective of how we fit into the total environment, and what we are doing to it and to ourselves, we are all doomed spiritually if not physically.

A Canyon Log

RODERICK NASH

ONCE AGAIN, the Canyon. Why did I return? Perhaps, most basically, for personal and intangible reasons. To re-experience the challenge of this place—the multifaceted challenge it poses to courage, aesthetic sensibility, and man's capacity for wonder. Certainly to get the feel of the Canyon country once again. To commune with time and power and process, and thereby to catch a glimpse of the meaning of the two billion years of earth's history on display here. To enroll in the next course in self-understanding that the university of the wilderness never fails to offer. But, in the last analysis, I came back because being in the Canyon is one of the world's great adventures.

The South Rim in predawn darkness: Ken Riley and I had arrived earlier than expected for our flight to Lee's Ferry, and to pass the time we drove to Mather Point. Thousands would stop here later in the day, but at 3 A.M. the parking lot was deserted. The moonless night robbed us of vision, yet the presence of the abyss rolled up in waves and from time to time a deep grumble reminded us of the river a mile below. Gradually, imperceptibly, the closest spurs and terraces swam into sight. Gray replacing black. You turned away momentarily, and when you looked back there was more and more and still more. Finally it was all there, vast, dimensionless in the flat light before sunup. It was as if the Grand Canyon had been created in a half-hour before our eyes—a high-speed rerun of ten million years.

From the air, as from the river, the Canyon is unbelievable. At our request the pilot of our single-engine plane dipped far below the rims to fly just above the inner gorge. As he made S-turns around buttes and spires, the incredible landscape unfolded. Details blurred, yet there was regularity to the pattern. Side canyon and spur; terrace and talus slope. The sculpture of erosion. After a hundred miles, we climbed high over the slot of Marble Gorge. The Vermilion Cliffs hemmed in the level plain of Marble Platform to the west; the Echo Cliffs to the east. Far to the north loomed the hulk of Navajo Mountain and pointing toward it, like an arrow, the blue streak of Lake Powell. Banking for the dirt runway near Lee's Ferry, we had a sudden glimpse down a side canyon, Soap Creek, and the toy waves of the rapid it created. We would soon know the fallacy of this airborn conception as we retraced in watery weeks the course we had covered in air-borne minutes. We would also come to know that the appropriate time span for even beginning to understand the Canyon is a lifetime.

Men write various names on maps, but there is no doubt that the geographical and aesthetic entity that is the Grand Canyon begins a mile below Lee's Ferry, where the Kaibab limestone first appears. The walls closed in, rose, then towered above our drifting boats. At Navajo Bridge, only six miles from Lee's the rim was already 467 feet above the river, the bridge a string of steel across the sky. We were locked into the trip until Grand Wash Cliffs, about 280 miles downstream. The Canyon would be our universe.

Evidence that it is a living, growing one was all around us. Below Navajo Bridge the river bends sharply to the left, and at the point of the turn a huge rockfall occurred a century, perhaps a millennium ago. The exposed rock, at any rate, has not acquired the coat of desert varnish that darkens the older cliffs. The talus, too, is white—a great fan of house-sized boulders extending right into the water. In other places erosion works more subtly, smoothing graceful water-cut grooves into the walls. Thus the Canyon widens even as it is deepened by the Colorado.

In camp early at Salt Water Wash below Soap Creek Rapids, we walked back to the plunging waters, staring, mesmerized, at the leaping waves. How does the rapid retain its form while the water that composes it rushes through? From high above, at the foot of the sheer wall, the waves in Soap no longer seethed; they seemed frozen in glittering steel.

Yesterday we moved too quickly, talked too loudly, strutted and postured. We were still in tune with civilization, still attempting to assert our insignificant egos against the Canyon's presence. But our inward pace soon slowed. It helped to inflate the kayak and drift in front of the main party. Without guidance the little boat spun slowly in the current, affording a complete view of Marble Gorge. At Twenty-one Mile Rapids I slipped down the tongue, bobbed over the standing waves, and spun into the downstream eddy, rejoicing in the ease with which the superbly buoyant craft handled the turbulence. I was falling back into older rhythms.

The walls now were massive Redwall that water and time have molded into magnificence. At Vaysey's Paradise, in the heart of Marble Gorge, a spring of cold clear water gushes directly out of the sheer wall several hundred feet above the river. Moss and ferns splash a patch of vivid green on the red cliff. But the scenic climax of Marble Gorge comes a little more than a mile downstream, where the Colorado makes a mile-long U-turn between sheer walls 1500 feet high. At the bottom of the U, the river has cut into the cliff on the outside of the turn. The result: an enormous cave. When the river fell with further cutting of the main channel, Redwall Cavern was left dry with a floor of fine sand. It must be 600 feet long, 300 deep, and 200 high. Our fire scarcely illuminated the cavern's dark recesses. The place was rich with evidence of the river's power. It was a good place to begin our education in the ways of water, time, and rock.

Kayak time again. I moved ahead of the boats, shooting some minor rapids but for the most part gliding smoothly on the living carpet of the Colorado. It is a magic one too, carrying me around bend after bend to wonder upon wonder. The Canyon below Redwall Cavern is unrivaled, to my mind, on the entire run. The walls are sheer, brilliantly red, and often eroded into double- and triple-decked arches and alcoves. The scale is titanic, the silence between rapids profound. At one point I heard, faintly, the sound of falling water but saw none. Paddling up-stream and down, I determined where the source was, then eased close to the seemingly solid wall. A tiny window revealed a miniature garden of delicate ferns watered by the tinkling source of the sound. There must have been another opening higher up because the scene was bathed in re-reflected light. Did Powell see this place? Has anyone? In the Canyon it is still easy to be a discoverer.

Moving swiftly in the kayak, I reached Mile 36, the site proposed for the Marble Gorge dam, considerably ahead of the main party. Two dark-mouthed tunnels broke the expanse of Redwall, and a tenuous scaffolding reached a third of the way up the inner gorge. Cautiously, I climbed to its top. Far above, the cable used by the Bureau of Reclamation engineers to ferry supplies from the outer rim flashed intermittently in the sun. If a dam were built at this point on the Colorado, it would impound water all the way to the foot of Glen Canyon Dam. Vaysey's Paradise, Redwall Cavern, and my concealed miniature garden would be drowned under hundreds of feet of water. Badger, Soap, Houserock, Twenty-five Mile, and Sheer Wall Rapids, to name a few, would be stilled; the river stripped of its eroding power. Such considerations have, thus far, helped block the dam. But the scaffolding still stands and so, presumably do the propo-nents of Marble Canyon Dam because this part of Marble Canyon is not pro-tected in a national park.* The present boundary, for no logical reason, is eleven river miles below the dam site and fifty miles from Lee's Ferry, where it should be.

The national park does begin at Nankoweap Creek. The well-preserved Indian ruins here are at the foot of the sheer wall. A scrambling climb of a half-mile up the talus brings you to them and to a splendid vista down a straight section of several miles of river. Directly beneath, the boats are dots on the sandbar below the swinging S-curve of Nankoweap Rapid. There are ruins like these through-out the Grand Canyon, the remains of civilizations that lived there as early as about 2000 B.C. The casual river runner sees perhaps a half-dozen evidences of Indian occupation. As recently as 1966, however, a team of anthropologists using a helicopter discovered more than two hundred sites.

Where Unkar Creek enters the Colorado across its wide delta, there is evidence of scholarship as well as Indians. Under permit from the National Park Service, a team of archeologists from several universities labored beneath a broiling sun to unearth the remains of a sizable community. The leaders of the dig received us warmly and explained how the Indians had apparently lived quite well on corn, squash, fish, and game. The scholars also lived well, with neat white tents, batteries of Coleman stoves, and even a volley-ball court beside the river on a gravel bar.

The twenty-five miles below Unkar constitute one of the most challenging stretches of navigable white water in the world. Any tougher and the rapids would be impassable. Hance, Sockdologer, Grapevine, Horn, Granite Falls, Her-

_____
* It is, however, in a newly created national monument. See page 107.

mit are legendary names in Grand Canyon lore. The boulder-carrying flood of 1967 has added a new one—Crystal. These rapids are eight, nine, and in some water conditions, ten on a ten-point scale of difficulty. We boomed through all of them in one fabulous day, pausing only at Phantom Ranch to leave mail and exposed film for the mules to tote up the Bright Angel Trail to the South Rim.

Starting just below Hance Rapid (Mile 76), the walls of the Upper Granite Gorge close in, rising straight from the water as limestone and sandstone give way to black Vishnu schist, estimated to be two billion years old, the original crust of the earth. Floating down the river we also drifted back through time until we reached beginnings. Here, on bedrock, one is forced to wonder anew about human endeavor. My personal confrontation came near our Tuna Creek camp. The spirit of the Canyon was brooding and somber, and the river still seethed restlessly from its shattering drop through mighty Crystal Rapid a mile upstream. Vaguely oppressed, I wandered out of camp across a bar littered with boulders. For some reason, I began to think about Maine's Mount Katahdin and a passage Henry David Thoreau wrote near its summit (quoted on page 32). The canyon, like Thoreau's mountain, had the power to strip away confidence in the spiritual symbolism of nature and in the divinity of man. What remained was rock-hard reality, an amoral nature—indifferent, older than thought, older than time. Sitting at the bottom of the darkening inner gorge, I mused on how recent and perilous an adventure thought itself is. The piece of schist I held now was far more than a thousand times older than any creature with a hand like mine, and older still than a mind that would be troubled by contemplating the age of either. These thoughts did not diminish my oppression. One must take such medicine in small doses, so I retreated quickly to camp, a drink, and the banter of men at their ease. Later on my sleeping bag, well fed, and with a pipe glowing warmly, I had reknit the mask with which we normally cover nature and I could think back to my moment of clairvoyance with some amusement. Yet I knew the Canyon had not changed. And I understood, at least to my satisfaction, why NASA astronauts preparing for a landing on the moon have trained in the Grand Canyon. Skill in climbing eroded rock believed similar to the moon's is not their only object. The astronauts must also develop the intellectual fortitude to face the ultimate reality of absolute wildness.

At Elves' Chasm we caught the Canyon in a different mood. Some thousands of years ago several huge boulders fell into and choked a side canyon down which a small clear stream poured. The result: a series of moss-covered grottoes cooled with a rainlike spray and in which river rapids echoed. The swimming was in well-tempered water, but to get back to the boats we had to cross talus slopes where our pocket thermometer stopped at 140 degrees—its maximum. We found it impossible to walk barefoot in sand exposed to direct sunlight or even to touch a dark rock.

With as much of the United States, excluding Alaska, paved today as is wild (about two percent each), it is highly unusual to walk where in all probability no one has ever walked before. Yet such places abound in Grand Canyon. One is Stone Creek. Winding down to join the Colorado from the Powell Plateau, a huge mesa isolated from the North Rim, Stone Creek possesses a delicate verdant beauty that strangers (including those who only stand on the rims) seldom associate with the Grand Canyon. The secret is water—a stream that originates in a spring under the plateau cuts a sharp slot through the limestone benches, supports rich meadows and large cottonwoods, plunges gracefully over travertine-laden waterfalls, and, some twelve miles later, loses its identity in the waters of the Colorado. Our trip was so scheduled as to allow Verne Huser, Peter Snow and me to ascend Stone Creek to its headwaters and camp overnight. We worked our way up eighty-foot falls, over piles of massive boulders, and through head-high grass and rushes. It gradually dawned on us that the imprints of our boots were probably unprecedented. Over our evening fire we contemplated with some awe and not a little pleasure that we were in one of the most isolated spots in the forty-eight contiguous states: to walk out to any kind of road would have required at least five hard days.

What is the worth to this country of places like Stone Creek? In dollars and cents, nothing—a fact which would-be developers of natural resources underscore. But for the human spirit, everything. Simply the *knowledge* that a portion of the earth exists in total wildness is a great possession.

While hiking up Stone Creek, we camped on a huge flat slab of rock directly in the creekbed but elevated about three feet. From this perch, perhaps 2,000 feet above the Colorado, the vastness of the Canyon was apparent in a way it seldom is at river level. Directly across from us the wall rose in tiers to the South Rim. On either side, and behind, was the giant bowl of the Stone Creek watershed. There were many choices, but I kept looking at the Redwall. Rather, I tried to look "into" the limestone and visualize the infinity of tiny organisms that had contributed their bodies to make this rock when it was the floor of an ancient sea. Then, looking deeper, I contemplated the great chain of living things as they have existed over time. My own place in that chain of life, and even of death, seemed explicable. A sense of cosmic contentedness, so different from the cosmic terror of Tuna Creek, swept in to perfect the evening.

The Grand Canyon is rich in side canyons. We passed dozens, the speed of the current permitting only a quick glance into their mouths; but a few had to be explored. One was the Tapeats Creek-Thunder River-Deer Creek complex. We ran the rapid in front of Tapeats, then walked back to its mouth. The first three casts in the clear, icy water produced three ten-inch rainbow trout that gleamed like polished silver. There were many more upstream, and as the party hiked along toward Thunder Springs I fell behind, exploring the deeper pools with a spinner. About two miles from the Colorado I found what I sought. As the lure sparkled down a chute of frothy water, a long dark shadow materialized behind it. At first I thought two or three of the small trout were trailing the lure. But when the line straightened and the spinner drifted out of the main flow, I realized this was a single enormous fish. A twitch of the rod tip darted the spinner ahead, and he was on! The next few minutes are a blur of motion and barked shins in my memory as the trout raced from pool to pool. Finally, there was the lip-biting suspense of sliding fingers under gills; then he was out—five pounds of Tapeats rainbow. Giving the fish to a friend (who convinced the group back at the boats he had caught it with his hands!), I hurried to catch the hikers at Thunder Springs. Our plan was to explore it, then climb out of Tapeats Canyon, cross five miles of relatively level esplanade, and descend Deer Creek to the Colorado. The boats, meanwhile, would run the three river miles between Tapeats and Deer and meet us at the end of the hike. It was easier and cooler on a map than on foot, and we didn't carry enough water, but six of us succeeded in measuring the Canyon with our legs and guts. We would no longer be deceived, by the ease of floating down the river, that this was easy country.

Each side creek in the Canyon seemed to have its own personality. Tapeats is a bright, dashing torrent. Deer runs relatively slowly through the heavy vegetation of Surprise Valley, then disappears in a slot only a yard wide before plunging 150 feet into the main river. Kanab is soft and languid. Soaking in one of its pools on a blisteringly hot day, I remained still for so long that minnows began to nibble my legs. An hour, two hours, who cared? It was a time to see the small things, a time to escape time. We camped this night on a series of ledges below Upset Rapid. It was a marvelous spot with a ledge for the kitchen, another for a bar, and one still higher for sleeping and eating. There was even a shower provided by the small stream descending from an amphitheater and cascading over one of the ledges in a convenient seven-foot fall.

At Havasu Creek we launched the kayak to reach the long pool behind the narrow entrance. The water of this stream, an astonishing turquoise where there is any depth, transforms its canyon into a symphony of light and color. It is possible to hike up Havasu Canyon to Supai, Arizona, the village home of 150 Havasupai Indians. The distance is eleven miles, and the trail skirts four spectacular waterfalls several hundred feet in height. Surely this beats the sixty-two mile dirt road drive from Route 66 and the eight-mile hike or mule ride required to reach Supai; but, as far as I know, only two persons have ever entered from the river side. Regrettably, we lacked the time to increase that number.

Everyone who runs the Colorado through Grand Canyon has a Lava Falls story. At Mile 179 the river encounters a series of lava boulders, and the result is a seething cauldron. One hole is of unprecedented size. Viewed from the talus above, there seems no way for a boat to come through upright. Sobered by this sight, we climbed quietly down to the neoprene rafts and battened down. The larger of our boats shot through successfully, if somewhat after the manner of an arrow released from a bow. But the smaller rig, composed of three ten-man rafts tied together, failed to climb out of Lava's notorious hole. The standing wave behind it was a full twenty feet high and steeply pitched, and the boat simply smashed against it and virtually stopped. With the full force of the river bearing down, the rearward raft folded under the front two. Then the entire rig seemed to go under. It emerged a few seconds later with men clinging to what holds they could find. Two, however, did not come up. Finally, after a heart-stopping

[81

half-minute, they burst through the downstream face of the great wave and made for shore. The boat was quickly reorganized and soon we were again floating the river, but with new respect.

Lava Falls is the last major rapid in the Canyon run. With it behind, I rigged the kayak and enjoyed thirty miles of superb paddling. One could sit and drift at the will of the current or paddle hard, adding five or six miles per hour to the river's four or five. At almost every bend I pulled onto a sandbar for a quick heat-beating swim. The only bad moment came in 217 Mile Rapids where the flow pounded squarely against the sheer sidewall before veering sharply to the right. Bouncing down the main flow, I did not see how I could avoid ramming the rock. But at the last moment the buffer wave, deflected from the solid surface, swung me safely downstream.

We elected to come off the river at Diamond Creek (Mile 225), just above the headwaters of Lake Mead, and the first place since Lee's Ferry where wheeled vehicles could reach the Colorado. Downstream, Lower Granite Gorge closed in again. We knew what we were missing: we would not, this time, feel the delicious damp coolness of Travertine Grotto or the chilling splash of Travertine Falls. We would not enjoy the grand tumultuous swim through the last rapids, at Mile 231, Mile 232, Mile 234, and Mile 237. We would have no chance, while passing the old Bureau of Reclamation camp near Bridge Canyon, to cheer the demise (for the moment) of the Hualapai dam project. And we would miss the bronze tablet marking the place where three of Powell's men climbed out of the Canyon to their deaths, at Separation Canyon. But we would also miss the miles of silt beds at the head of Lake Mead—and who would enjoy witnessing the death of the living Colorado?

If I were an American, I should make my remembrance of it the final test of men, art, and policies. I should ask myself: Is this good enough to exist in the same country as the Canyon? How would I feel about this man, this kind of art, these political measures, if I were near that Rim? Every member or officer of the Federal Government ought to remind himself, with triumphant pride, that he is on the staff of the Grand Canyon.   J. B. PRIESTLEY

Shooting the Wild Colorado

Stewart L. Udall

Every individual—and every family—should get to know at least one river. It might be an upland creek or a small stream that offers the intimate pleasure of fishing or swimming. It might be a middle size river that one can canoe, boat upon, or savor from hikes along its shores. Or it might be a long river or a turbulent tributary that winds through a majestic riverscape like the Allagash of Maine or the Salmon of Idaho.

The great river of my home region, the Colorado, falls in the last category. It rises in the high crests of the Rockies and plunges seaward fourteen hundred miles through the most varied and scenic landscape I know. The call of the Colorado has lured the Udalls across the continent four times in the past eight years. In 1960, with our two oldest children, Tom and Scott, we ran the soon-to-be-flooded Glen Canyon stretch of the river. A year later, accompanied by several Congressmen from Utah, we made a river-based survey of the wilderness country below Moab, which led to the creation of Canyonlands National Park. And in 1964 we took a boat camp-out trip on Lake Powell to visit the majestic Rainbow Bridge and the sculptured side canyons of the Escalante.

The supreme adventure of the Colorado, however, is the float trip from Lee's Ferry through Marble Gorge and the Grand Canyon itself to the waters of Lake Mead. Last summer was the right time for us to take the big trip. At age eight, Jamie, our youngest child, was old enough to go traveling on the river, and I was officially anxious to see those sections of it involved in the bitter dams and parks controversy then pending before Congress.

So, in mid-June, we found ourselves near the Utah border, poised on two pontoon rafts with friends, cousins, park officials and two river guides, ready for a once-in-a-lifetime outdoor experience. For nearly two weeks we would float through the climactic canyons of the Colorado, run some of the most turbulent rapids on the continent, camp on sandbars and sleep under the stars. We would also sever all contact with the outside world. (In my note to President Johnson advising him of my prolonged absence, I warned that I would be "unreachable . . . and off your radar screen.")

Nearly two million Americans travel to the edge of the Grand Canyon every year to gaze on this sculptured masterwork of wind and water. By general agreement, it is one of the finest "park experiences" in our country. However, the raft riders a mile down get a totally different and more intimate look at the great can-

Reprinted from *Venture, The Traveler's World*, February 1968; © 1968 by Travelventures, Inc.

yons. For one thing, the view from below is more personal, more involved: the river they ride is the knife that cut these canyons, the thunder at each rapid is the sound of the grinding stones of a great waterway. It is truly a ride on the wild side, for the Colorado plunges more than 2000 feet in a 240-mile stretch of river.

Our first day introduced us to the rapids, to our pontoon type rafts and to our river guides. The National Park Service licenses half a dozen professional rafters to run this section of the Colorado. Ours was Jack Currey, a crew-cut young Mormon from Salt Lake City whose rigs run western rivers nine months of the year. Like all real boatmen, Jack was an expert "reader" of rapids, a skilled open-fire cook, an able rig repairer and, in a pinch, an adequate medical corpsman. He was also a competent geographer, and invariably good-natured. (Nearness to water does something to men, I believe; it makes them people your children remember.)

We experienced many of the pleasures and risks of river travel during our first afternoon in Marble Gorge. We had two tranquil hours of floating and a stop for swimming on a small sandbar; we rafted by two booming rapids, picked a perfect campsite and ate sizzling steaks under a moon to watch stars by. The world we entered at Lee's Ferry was a composite of moving water, desert sunlight, colored canyons and occasional signs of wildlife. Each bend of the river altered the kaleidoscope: shadow patterns shifted as clouds floated by, and the walls of the gorge grew higher as new sandstone formations appeared.

This is the fascination of a river float: each bend brings change, the senses quicken, and conversation is punctuated with "Look . . . look!"—at new forms, new color combinations in the cliffs, new elements of an unfolding outdoors.

The abrupt drops at Badger Creek and Soap Creek gave us an exciting introduction to the big rapids. Waterfalls and rapids are two of nature's most awesome exhibitions; the main difference is that men *watch* waterfalls but can *ride* rapids. A great rapids is one of nature's classic clashes, for it pits the irresistible power of wild water against the nearly immovable force of unyielding rocks. In the long run, as the Grand Canyon attests, the water wins; but the short run is a furious standoff, with the special circumstances of each collision determining the height of the waves, the depth of the holes, the downward speed of the water—and the dimensions of the danger.

We learned many things about rapids and river safety that first afternoon in Marble Gorge. We learned to recognize the muffled rumble that announces an oncoming rapids, that a good, seasoned river guide always stops to reconnoiter the largest rapids and that he has enormous respect for their rolling waters.

For some reason I had anticipated an oar-guided float trip and was disappointed to find that each raft was powered by a small outboard motor. But Jack Currey explained that a true float would mean an extra week on the river. Later he demonstrated that the safe passage of a large raft rests on the pilot's ability to position it at the head of each rapids and maneuver in midpassage in order to "cheat" around the most dangerous boulders and holes. The other key to safety is a well secured life jacket—the one indispensable item of river attire.

As we watch Jack read the first rapids we begin to grasp the art, and peril, of river running. Rocks can puncture and wreck a raft, holes can overturn it. Here we are, gripping our individual anchor ropes, barreling down the tongue of Soap Creek into a two hundred yard maelstrom of churning froth. The jet force of the first ten-foot wave tosses the front end skyward; the raft shudders, seems suspended in midair, then dips downward as twisting crosswaves drench everything aboard. The pontoons are now a plaything of explosive water: the bronco action accelerates as the river pummels each raft with a left jab, a right cross, a stiff uppercut in quick combinations. This is no roller-coaster ride; waves, crosswaves, chutes and rocks make each moment a violent blur.

Jack's instruction sheet said, "Bring a hat you can tie on your head." The four of us who ignored this advice have lost our hats and caps at the first big rapids, but the ride leaves us too limp to worry about headgear. River runners have a 1-to-10 rating scale for rapids, but son Jamie has developed a much simpler system of his own: the smaller ones are "no hands" rapids, and the roar of the big ones make him shout "captains courageous!" as we race through the rough water.

For the first three days of our trip, the water was as clear as a mountain stream. But on the fourth morning we woke to find that a storm somewhere on the upper plateau had turned the great river a light brown. The sculptured rock that lines the riverbanks has been burnished by the scouring action of the silt. The inner gorge of the Grand Canyon is a paradise for geologists, sculptors and photographers. Nowhere else on earth can one witness such a fantastic display of water-worn rock, for nowhere else are rock strata of the earliest period of time so exposed to the scrutiny of man.

The stretch of river we traversed contains about seventy rapids. The big ones like Bedrock, Vulcan [or Lava Falls—ED.], Hancy, Dubendorff, Upset, all remain vivid in my mind. We will particularly remember Soap Creek (where we first learned how rapid a big rapids can be), Twenty-five Mile (where one of our group was thrown overboard), Granite (where a last-second twist by the outboard saved us), Upset (where we missed a huge hole and hit a rock) and Vulcan (the last and fastest of the big ones).

But the Colorado contains much more than rapids. There are other adventures; and if the risks are fewer, the outdoor experience is still enormously satisfying. The exploring of side canyons is one of the special delights of this river. We gloried in our swim in the turquoise water of the Little Colorado, as we did in our hike to the Elves' Chasm, in our camp in the thunder of Deer Creek Falls (a waterfall in the desert is sheer poetry) and in our two hour walk up Havasu Canyon. On summer days wildlife is scarce in desert canyons; to sight a chuckwalla, a water ouzel, a wild burro or a great blue heron is a satisfying experience.

Time and again this pristine country makes the voyager feel he is the first human being to stand on a certain spot. There is a sense of reverence as one idles on a small beach of purest sand disturbed only by the track of a lone bird, a lizard, a snake. The floor of this canyon is nature at her most inviolate.

Our trip was more than a physical encounter with a wild river. Reliving the past is also adventure, and this section of the Colorado has a rich story to tell of prehistoric times and of the period of pioneer settlement. The day before we began our raft ride we spent several hours at Lee's Ferry, a settlement founded by my great-grandfather John D. Lee. This was the only site on the river for nearly five hundred miles where wagons and cattle could be moved southward into the Territory of Arizona. The children marveled at the sturdy, primitive buildings Lee built. We then crossed the river and hiked up the trail where our Arizona-bound relatives hauled their wagons over the high ridge they called Lee's Backbone. The still visible ruts cut by the wagon wheels, and the rock embankments of the "dugways" built by these Mormon pioneers, made everyone in our party appreciate the hardships of frontier travel.

Our visit to prehistoric Indian ruins in the bottom of Grand Canyon was a backward leap into history. Shards of pottery, and the foundations of ancient dwellings uncovered by archeologists, unfolded part of the story of the first Americans who settled in these forbidding canyons. A boy who finds pieces of pots shaped by human hands six centuries ago truly has something to ponder.

We were retracing the final stretch of the river ride taken by the Major John Wesley Powell Expedition of 1869—the last great adventure in the exploration of the West. Powell's journal, read aloud around the campfire, helped us relive the fears and hopes of his team. (One entry in his diary, written as his small wooden boats approached the Grand Canyon, was filled with foreboding: "We are three-quarters of a mile in the depths of the earth, and the great river shrinks into insignificance. . . . We have an unknown distance yet to run; an unknown river yet to explore. What falls there are, we know not; what rocks beset the channel, we know not.") Powell, who lost an arm at the Battle of Shiloh, shared the same daring spirit that took Lewis and Clark across the continent. We could only marvel at the fortitude that carried him and his ten men in their fragile boats through the wild water of the Colorado.

Besides adventure, the Colorado trip gave me a firsthand look at the canyons involved in the dispute between the dam builders and the conservation groups spearheaded by the Sierra Club. It taught me once again that the Secretary of the Interior should never make armchair judgments on national conservation issues.

I can confess now that I approached this problem with a less-than-open mind in early 1963, when we began our planning at Interior for the Lower Colorado Project. I knew that Arizona's underground water was being used up at an alarming rate and that traditional policy required a hydro dam to provide the electric power for pumping water over the hill to the arid valley of my home state.

This was all changed in January of 1967, when Interior experts, after a four month study, produced a no-dam solution to Arizona's water problem that won the support of the White House. Under the new plan, electricity to pump water over the hill to the central valley would come from a coal-fired steam plant, not a hydro dam. The cost of the project would be drastically reduced, and so would the controversy. Once this was proposed, the country and Congress were free to reexamine all the values of the Colorado from Lee's Ferry to Lake Mead.

We recommended that the Marble Gorge dam not be built; there now seems to be a conservation consensus that this canyon should be added to the Grand Canyon National Park. However, the dispute over the downriver Hualapai Dam (previously called Bridge Canyon Dam) remains; our report urged that a decision be deferred pending evaluation by a national water commission to be appointed by the President. Hualapai would back water twenty-seven miles through the Grand Canyon National Monument (created by a presidential proclamation in 1932) and thirteen miles into the national park (created by an act of Congress in 1919). Hualapai, experts say, is a first-rate site for a hydro dam, but preservationists ardently insist that this lower section of the Grand Canyon also be kept unimpaired. In Washington I had read all the arguments on both sides. Now, as we floated by, the canyons could speak for themselves. Turning southward where the river bends at Kanab Creek, I felt fresh doubts about hasty decisions concerning this reach of the Colorado, for it is not duplicated upstream. From Kanab Creek to Toroweap the inner gorge takes on a new aspect: the walls become sheer, and the cathedral effect of a three thousand foot, multihued sandstone escarpment is overpowering. Havasu Creek, with its cascades and deep side canyons, is a sensational sideshow, the closest thing to Shangri-La in the canyon. I realized then that the park experts who drew the boundaries for the National Monument were trying to preserve exceptional features of the Grand Canyon.

The Hualapai Dam would consume, not conserve, water. This is beyond dispute. But many conservationists still argue that a recreation lake in the particular canyon would be superior to a scenic river. However, even here I was skeptical as our raft navigated the narrow canyon. The value of a manmade lake is measured by its surface size, the area available for water play, the fish life it sustains, the miles of shoreline it creates, the areas where public access can be provided, the number of side canyons in which boaters can camp and explore. Hualapai falls short on all accounts. If one uses a 1-to-10 rating scale, Lake Powell must get a score of 9, Lake Mead 8, and the lake behind Hualapai 1. A chart tells the story:

	Water acres	Shoreline miles	Good access points
Lake Powell	161,000	1,900	8
Lake Mead	158,000	500	16
Hualapai Reservoir	16,700	200	1

There is one final problem at Hualapai that deserves careful evaluation. The most silt-laden tributaries of the Colorado are the Paria, the Little Colorado and Kanab Creek. They drain the badlands and eroded deserts of the Colorado Plateau above the site of the Hualapai dam. When the rainstorms come to this region the land surrenders topsoil without a struggle; the result is that such a reservoir would fill up with silt so fast (some say in 160 years, some 250) that the lake's "life" would be seriously shortened.

The possibility of a compromise in this section of the river is limited: if hydropower dictates that a dam be built, a high dam, not a half dam, should be constructed. On the other hand, if a hydro dam is not really needed, the boundaries of the Grand Canyon National Park should be changed.

The burden of proof, I believe, rests on the dam builders. If they cannot make out a compelling case, the park should be enlarged and given permanent protection.

*You never tire of trying to understand how the river did it,
chiseling, smoothing, bringing new forms out of the old stone,
when its only tools are living water and finest sand.*

The round earth turns and follows its course among the stars.
The river unearths the ancient rock laid down many cataclysms ago.

The water dissolves limestone, paving the ancient rock with it
where thin streams and seeps of limewater lay down travertine.

Grand Canyon National Monument protects some remnants of a time when
lava poured out over the rim country, filling side canyons,
boiling into the river and plugging it. Volcanic tapestries
and columns of basalt along miles of the canyon below the Monument
are vestiges of the tumult John Wesley Powell imagined:

"*a river of molten rock running down into a river of melted snow . . .*
What a seething of the waters, what clouds of steam!"
The heat that melted rocks is now just enough to keep some springs warm.
Earth's fire, though banked, is not dead in the Grand Canyon.
Nothing is. The Canyon lives.

The talus and the sandbars let the flowers, grass, and cactus live,
and the animals that let us see them, and those that do not.
The river itself, urgent and coherent, is alive, and there is magic in it.

Down deep in the earth that the river has already delved a mile into
you see the life in stone Loren Eiseley wrote about:
"The huge stones were beasts, I used to think, of a kind
man ordinarily lived too fast to understand. They seemed inanimate
because the tempo of the life in them was slow. They lived ages
in one place and moved only when man was not looking.
Sometimes at night I would hear a low rumble as one drew itself
into a new position and subsided again."

The cycle of life goes on.
The Colorado River and Grand Canyon live;
and in our intimate connection with them, we live.

Like all great things, the Canyon takes time to appreciate. So be wary of your companion's instant rhapsody of applause. Be more wary of that sacred hush affected by others. Simply take your look, turn on your heel and leave. The Canyon will be there if you ever return.

FRANK WATERS

THE PEOPLE'S CANYON

Backpackers and boatmen come to know the Grand Canyon in special ways; so do those who ride mules down and up the established trails. Even Rim-watchers fall under the spell of this place. But ultimately the Canyon belongs to the people as a whole. Everyone everywhere has a stake in the Grand Canyon and a right to see it—or simply to think about it—in its natural condition. And the right extends to those yet unborn. By a stroke of geographical good fortune, Americans count the Canyon in their territorial limits. But possession entails responsibility; we hold the Grand Canyon in trust for all mankind. One of the ways history will judge our civilization is by examining our execution of this charge.

To set up a national park or a wilderness area is to establish a limit, to say "thus far and no farther" to development. If we cannot prosper without a dam or mine or lumber operation within the designated area of wilderness, then we must simply limit prosperity to this extent and acknowledge that the good life may be reached at a point short of the full economic utilization of every resource on the planet. We put other considerations before growth. We redefine "progress" to include preservation and appreciation as well as development.

For Americans especially, such self-limitation does not come easily. One hallmark of our national character is a thirst and a talent for conquering nature: this drive came over on the Mayflower, went west in covered wagons, and now seeks new worlds among the stars. Its accomplishments are indisputable, but so are its dangers. The point is to make a place alongside the pride we take in man's works for humility in the face of nature's. If we can understand Grand Canyon and places like it as cultural, not natural, resources, valuable simply because they are there, we will have made a giant leap in this regard.—ED.

The Perils and Possibilities of a Park

RODERICK NASH

THE NATIONAL PARK IDEA is one of America's original contributions to world civilization. We have had our faults as a people, and perhaps the Russians actually beat us to Coca-Cola, but our invention of national parks is an encouraging and indisputable fact. The establishment of Yellowstone National Park on March 1, 1872, was the world's first instance of large-scale wilderness preservation in the public interest. Subsequently we created other national parks, including that which protects a portion of the Grand Canyon, and we exported the institution around the world. Japan, New Zealand, and several African nations have acknowledged our leadership and sought our advice. In 1919 King Albert of Belgium visited Yosemite, Grand Canyon, and Yellowstone, then returned home determined to implement preservation in his country. England's national parks stemmed from a visit to this country by Lord Bledisloe. So great was the demand for information in the 1960s that the National Park Service, in cooperation with several private conservation groups, insituted a summer course in national park administration for foreigners. By 1969, the four-week program had enrolled participants from fifty-one countries.

We are, then, admired and envied for our wilderness and our parks. But all too often our criteria have been biased in favor of changing the landscape, and the parks, like prophets, have gone without honor in the land of their birth.

Grand Canyon is a case in point. Americans have endeavored to build copper mines and private resorts in it, railroads through it, tramways down it, and, in wild flights of fancy, cable cars across it rim to rim. Schemes for exploitation appeared in the 1880s, and they continue today despite the growth to major proportions of the American wilderness preservation movement.* In the middle of the 1960s a proposal to build dams on the Colorado River in Grand Canyon missed enactment by an eyelash. And the possibility of dams still imperils the Canyon. Embarrassingly, when the controversy over the dams was at its height, a participant from India in the summer park administration course stood on the South Rim and remarked softly, "The Grand Canyon is more than American—it should be preserved for all the world." We should not have to be reminded. The mere existence of this place should be enough to save it unspoiled for everyone for all time. Yet in this respect even the Canyon has failed. Grand Canyon National Park still awaits completion.

* For a full discussion of the changing American attitude toward wilderness see the author's *Wilderness and the American Mind* (New Haven, Yale University Press, 1967).

The history of man's effort to protect the Grand Canyon as a scenic resource began in 1882 when Benjamin Harrison, as Senator from Indiana, introduced a bill in the 47th Congress to establish a public park in the area. Coming only a decade after Yellowstone and eight years before Yosemite National Park's creation, Harrison's idea was a bold departure from usual land policy in the Gilded Age. This may have been its undoing. The Harrison bill died without even reaching a floor vote. In 1893 Benjamin Harrison, as President, had another chance. An unprecedented act of Congress in 1891 empowered the chief executive to create forest reserves (later renamed national forests) by withdrawing land from the public domain. Harrison seized the opportunity, and two years later proclaimed fifteen reserves totaling more than 13 million acres, the Grand Canyon among them. Since the forest reserve act did not specify the function of the withdrawn areas, John Muir, president of the Sierra Club, and the handful of Americans in favor of preserving wilderness thought they had won a great victory. But it soon became apparent that others, notably Gifford Pinchot, regarded the reserves as opportunities for planned development of resources rather than preservation.

By 1898, with Pinchot heading the federal forest management program, Muir had abandoned hope for the forest reserves and was calling for more national parks. In an article of that year in *Atlantic Monthly* he described the Grand Canyon in the emotional language he usually reserved for his beloved Sierra: "No matter how far you have wandered hitherto, or how many famous gorges or valleys you have seen, this one, the Grand Cañon of the Colorado, will seem as novel to you . . . as if you had found it after death, on some other star." Muir concluded his essay with a plea to make the Canyon a national park.

Muir's *Atlantic* article of 1898 was symptomatic of and contributory to the growing attention paid the West's spectacular natural beauty on the part of tourists. To serve the demand the Santa Fe Railroad constructed a spur line to the South Rim of the Canyon in 1901. The number of visitors increased so sharply in the next few years that the construction of the El Tovar Hotel became appropriate. One of those who came, looked, and marveled was Theodore Roosevelt. A historian before entering the political arena, Roosevelt realized that the American frontier was vanishing and that, lacking wilderness, Americans might lose the pioneer characteristics that underlay their greatness. As President in 1903 Roosevelt was in a position to do more than regret; consequently his remarks of that year in a speech on the South Rim (quoted on page 108) gave promise of action.

In 1906 Roosevelt signed a bill establishing the Grand Canyon National Game Preserve. Then on January 11, 1908, he used the authority granted him under the Antiquities Act to designate the central portion of Grand Canyon a national monument. As such is was officially protected for its historic and scientific value (that is, its possession of ancient Indian ruins), but there is no doubt Roosevelt had more in mind. The Grand Canyon National Monument of 1908 was his way of protecting a superlative piece of wilderness until Congress made up its mind to accord it the national park status he knew it deserved.

In the decade after 1908 the Grand Canyon was divided into a crazy-quilt pattern of land administration units. Along with the national monument, two sections of national forest and a portion of the old game preserve existed in the region. Indian reservations further complicated the picture. Farsighted legislators saw the need for unified administration. In 1911, for instance, Representative Everis A. Hayes of California tried to have the Canyon designated Carnegie National Park in honor of the steel tycoon and philanthropist. Others thought that if a national park were created, it should bear the name of the first man through by boat, John Wesley Powell. But the chief concern was the Canyon, not its name, and gradually a movement for national park status gained momentum. The Sierra Club, the Department of the Interior, Arizona Congressmen, and the Santa Fe Railroad (which by 1915 was servicing most of the 100,000 annual visitors) advanced the park idea. Finally on February 26, 1919, President Woodrow Wilson signed a bill establishing Grand Canyon National Park. Most of the land in the game preserve and the 1908 national monument was included, but at least a million acres of the Canyon were not.

As a national park the protected part of the Grand Canyon became part of a system created under the National Park Act of 1916. In the language of this law, the purpose of national parks was "to conserve the scenery and the natural and historic objects and the wild life therein, and to provide for the enjoyment of the same in such manner and by such means as will leave them unimpaired for the enjoyment of future generations." But in the case of the Grand Canyon the lawmakers of 1919 compromised this ideal by allowing the Secretary of the Interior to grant railroad rights of way through the park and to authorize federal reclamation projects on the Colorado River within it, whenever consistent with the primary purposes of the park. Given the Canyon's geography, railroads were never much of a threat but dams were something else.

In the early years of the monument and park, however, the major peril came in the person of Ralph Henry Cameron, an Arizona political boss. It occurred to Cameron that if he could gain control of the major trails, springs, and choice overlooks, he could make a killing on the tourist trade. For a time things seemed to be going Cameron's way. Just before Roosevelt established the monument, Cameron located dozens of land claims at strategic places along the South Rim. A toll station soon appeared on the Bright Angel Trail, exacting a dollar from everyone who passed up or down. At Indian Gardens, a lovely spring on the trail midway between Rim and river, Cameron ran a "resort" so expensive and filthy that few cared to stay. He also charged exorbitant rates for the use of his restrooms and refused to relent even when implored by lady travelers who had left their money at the Rim. In addition, Cameron clung to some eighty mining claims and various dam sites in the Canyon. The fact that he was elected United States Senator from Arizona in 1920 made his dislodgement from the new park difficult. In time, however, better men came to the Canyon and gradually liquidated Cameron's empire. The episode was a lesson in the need for national parks.

In 1932, in recognition of the scientific value of the great lava flows in the western part of the Canyon, President Herbert Hoover created the second Grand Canyon National Monument, immediately west (downstream) from the national park. Pressure was put on the National Park Service to assure the Bureau of Reclamation that dam building was not precluded in the monument, but the Presidential proclamation contained no such provision. At the time the point seemed academic because the reclamationists had as much as they could handle completing Hoover Dam lower on the Colorado. There were also plenty of hydropower opportunities above Grand Canyon, and in 1956 the Colorado River Storage Project authorized four major dams. Flaming Gorge Dam was built on the Green River above Dinosaur National Monument, which its friends saved from inundation after an all-out fight against dams proposed at Echo Park and Split Mountain.* Curecanti on the Gunnison and Navajo on the San Juan were also constructed under the 1956 legislation. And on the main Colorado just above Lee's Ferry, Glen Canyon Dam created Lake Powell.† As these projects neared completion, the Bureau of Reclamation took another look at the 300 miles of undeveloped river between Lake Mead and Lake Powell. The idea of building dams in Grand Canyon was not new. Two sites in particular had long been known: at Bridge Canyon and in Marble Gorge, both within Grand Canyon. Both places had been fully surveyed in the 1920s as part of the process that resulted in the selection of Boulder Canyon as the site of Hoover Dam. And a bill authorizing construction of a dam at Bridge Canyon had actually passed the Senate in 1950, only to be summarily defeated in the House. There were also elaborate plans of long standing to bring water from a reservoir in Marble Canyon through a forty-mile tunnel under the Kaibab Plateau to hydropower facilities in Kanab Creek. Ninety percent of the Colorado would have been diverted from its normal course through Grand Canyon.

The Grand Canyon dam controversy, one of the classic confrontations in the history of American conservation, began to gather momentum in 1963 when Secretary of the Interior Stewart L. Udall made public the Bureau of Reclamation's billion-dollar Pacific Southwest Water Plan. Its scope was unprecedented: to solve the growing Southwest's water shortage, the reclamationists proposed diverting water from Northern California or the Columbia River and transporting it in a series of tunnels, ducts, and canals to the Lower Colorado Basin. The increased flow would be utilized with the aid of a series of new dams and diversion facilities. One of the latter, the Central Arizona Project, called for transporting water from Lake Havasu on the lower Colorado to the booming Phoenix-Tucson area. To finance this and generate power to move the water to Central Arizona, dams would be built at Bridge and Marble canyons, within Grand Canyon.

* For a description of what was at stake in the Echo Park controversy and an analysis of the struggle itself see Wallace Stegner, ed., *This Is Dinosaur: Echo Park Country and Its Magic Rivers* (New York, Alfred A. Knopf, 1955); Roderick Nash, *Wilderness and the American Mind* (New Haven, Yale University Press, 1967), pp. 209–219; and *The Echo Park Controversy*, by Philip Sirotkin and Owens S. Stratton (University of Alabama, 1959).

† Belatedly, conservationists recognized the superlative qualities of a wild Glen Canyon and tried unsuccessfully to block the dam. See David Brower, ed., *The Place No One Knew: Glen Canyon on the Colorado* (San Francisco, Sierra Club, 1963).

The proposed Marble Canyon Dam would flood fifty-three miles of river—the lower part of Glen Canyon and the upper Grand Canyon. The dam at Bridge Canyon would back water up for ninety-three miles including forty in Grand Canyon National Monument and thirteen along the northwestern edge of the national park. Eventually, sedimentation would encroach still further on the park and monument. The Bureau of Reclamation anticipated the opposition of wilderness preservationists and constructed a scale model of the Grand Canyon for the purpose of showing that the dams and reservoirs would not impair scenic values. Indeed, the Bureau contended, the lakes would permit millions to enjoy the little-known beauties of the inner canyon in comparative safety. Such arguments and the official backing of Secretary Udall and the Lyndon B. Johnson administration led most observers to expect that the dams would be approved in the 89th Congress. This impression was further supported by the tenor of Congressional hearings in 1965 and 1966. But on June 9, 1966, a now-famous advertisement (see page 133) appeared on full pages of the *New York Times* and the *Washington Post*. The Sierra Club had chosen this means of explaining the threat to the Grand Canyon and arousing public protest. The $15,000 ad paid remarkable dividends. Mail deploring Bridge and Marble Canyon Dams poured into key Washington offices. Senator Thomas Kuchel of California termed the conservationists' effort "one of the largest letter-writing campaigns which I have ever seen." But the greatest success of the ad was unexpected: on June 10, the day after it appeared, the Internal Revenue Service warned the Sierra Club that henceforth it could no longer guarantee the deductibility of donations to the club. In the opinion of the IRS, the club was engaging in "substantial" efforts to influence legislation, which the law did not permit tax-exempt organizations to do. By clouding the club's tax status, this action—as the IRS must have anticipated— immediately cut off many major contributions to the club.

If the warning of the IRS was designed to help the cause of the dam builders, it was a backfire of colossal proportions. In the public mind, at least, it appeared that the Sierra Club was being punished by the administration, which at the time supported the dams, for altruistic efforts on behalf of Grand Canyon. It was clear, at any rate, that other tax-deductible organizations carried on vigorous lobbying programs without incurring IRS displeasure. The Sierra Club's advertisement had appeared on an interior page of two newspapers; the IRS charge became front-page news across the country. People who didn't know or care about the threat to Grand Canyon as wilderness now rose on its behalf in the name of civil liberties. Could the government intimidate citizen protest? Were only well-connected activists tolerated? The tax action made the issue of the dams transcend conservation, and prompted protest letters from thousands who might never have written about the Canyon alone.

With the tide of national opinion running in their favor, defenders of the Canyon pressed their case. The Sierra Club on July 25, 1966, placed another full-page ad in the *New York Times* (see page 137). Later in the summer a number of newspapers and national magazines carried still a third (see page 139). The gist of the preservationists' argument was simple: the Grand Canyon was one of the world's special places; it should be saved in its natural condition. In answer to the Bureau of Reclamation's argument that the dams would not even be visible from most places on the Rims, the opposition replied that it was essential on emotional grounds to know that the free-flowing, living river that had cut the chasm was still at work. Dams, moreover, would eliminate the possibility of one of the world's supreme adventures: running the Colorado by boat through Grand Canyon.

Supporting these points was the charge that the Grand Canyon dams served no purpose other than to finance a massive water plan. Was the United States so poor, conservationists wondered, that it had to exploit the Grand Canyon in order to pay for a water supply? Coal-fired thermal plants or nuclear generators could supply the requisite power at less cost than the dams. Another line of attack stemmed from the evidence that the dams would actually waste the Colorado's limited supply of water through evaporation and seepage. In this way the dams were represented as working against the very purpose of the Pacific Southwest Water Plan and the Central Arizona Project.

As a result of the previous summer's furor, reclamationists brought revised proposals to the January 1967 opening of the 90th Congress. They would abandon Marble Canyon Dam entirely. But Bridge Canyon (renamed "Hualapai") Dam would remain, and, in order to avoid trespassing on a part of the national park system, Grand Canyon National Monument would be abolished. Preservationists were not receptive. One bullet in the heart, they maintained, was just as deadly as two. And changing names on a map did not alter the fact that a dam was being placed in the Grand Canyon. Adding greatly to the preservation cause at this time were two potent weapons: François Leydet's *Time and the River Flowing: Grand Canyon,* which appeared in the Sierra Club's Exhibit Format Series to strengthen the point that the mistake made in Glen Canyon should not be repeated downstream in Grand, and two 25-minute, sound-and-color motion pictures by the Sierra Club: "The Grand Canyon," which dramatized the same message, and "Glen Canyon," which powerfully portrayed a major loss of canyon wilderness that was about to be compounded.

On February 1, 1967, the dam builders' hopes plunged when Secretary Udall announced that the Johnson administration had changed its mind about the Grand Canyon dams. For the time being, Udall suggested, the Central Arizona Project should plan to receive its money and pumping power from a thermal-powered plant.* Meanwhile, the Sierra Club kept up the antidam momentum with another full-page advertisement on March 13 (see page 141) warning Americans of the danger that remained in a one-dam proposal. Washington mail boxes again filled, and the pressure began to tell. In June the Senate Interior and Insular Affairs Committee voted to authorize the Central Arizona Project without either of the controversial dams. The Committee also took steps to preclude the possibility that either the state of Arizona or the city of Los Angeles would build a dam in the Canyon on its own initiative. On August 8, 1967, the Senate followed its Committee's recommendation and passed a damless Central Arizona Project.

In the House, however, Representative Wayne Aspinall of Colorado, chairman of the Interior and Insular Affairs Committee and a pro-dam stalwart, continued to fight. But by early 1968 even proponents of Bridge Canyon Dam saw the writing on the wall. Morris K. Udall, Congressman from Arizona, announced in January that even if his state tried to "go it alone" in procuring water, there would be no attempts to build dams in the Grand Canyon. Congressman Udall was not happy about losing the dam fight, but he was realistic. "I must tell you bluntly," he declared, "that no bill providing for a so-called 'Grand Canyon dam' can pass the Congress today."

On July 31, 1968, House and Senate conferees on the Central Arizona Project bill rang the death knell on Grand Canyon dams. The text they agreed upon included the following sentences: ". . . nothing in this section or in this Act contained shall be construed to authorize the study or construction of any dams on the main stream of the Colorado River between Hoover Dam and Glen Canyon Dam." And ". . . the Federal Power Act shall not be applicable to the reaches of the main stream of the Colorado between Hoover Dam and Glen Canyon Dam until and unless otherwise provided by Congress."

The second stipulation simply meant that the ability of the Federal Power Commission to sanction dams on the nation's rivers would not apply to the Colorado in Grand Canyon. A special act of Congress would be required for any private or governmental organization to build a dam in this area. While it was and is possible that such an act could be passed, the sentiment of the American people and their government is at present such as to make this highly unlikely.

American conservation turned a significant corner when, on September 30, 1968, President Johnson signed a damless Central Arizona Project bill into law. Dams that at one point had enjoyed the full backing of his administration, the personal support of the Secretary of the Interior, and the almost unanimous support of Senators and Representatives from the seven Colorado Basin states, as well as the energetic boosting of water and power users' associations and their lobbies—dams, in other words, that seemed virtually certain of authorization— were blocked. And the blocking force was not a well-heeled and well-placed lobby but private conservation organizations and concerned citizens united only by a determination to SAVE GRAND CANYON, as their bumper stickers declared. Yet this was no minor power. "Hell," as a Congressman who preferred anonymity remarked shortly after the Grand Canyon dam controversy, "has no fury like a conservationist aroused."

It would be an injustice to end here with the credits for saving the Canyon. Many other conservation organizations worked as hard as they could in the face of the adverse IRS action against the Sierra Club—action the club could withstand because of its varied sources of revenue (membership, publications, wilderness outings, and grants) but which organizations wholly dependent upon deductible contributions could not risk. There were the individuals, too, who responded from many places and disciplines and made major presentations, in writing, on the air, or, traveling to Washington at their own expense, in testimony before the

* For Secretary Udall's personal description of his change of mind, see pages 83–7.—Ed.

Congressional committees. What concerned them was the Grand Canyon. There was no other Grand Canyon. And then there was the delegation from the Pacific Northwest. The prospect of seeing their Columbia River sent southward to water cotton, smog, and votes in southern California and Arizona did not please them. True, the Columbia was a big river, but they had their own plans for it, including a wish to keep it running in its own channel for the purposes for which it was put there in the first place. Part of the defense of the Columbia was a new concept of planning for water use that challenged many of the traditions of dam-and-ditch thinking that had traditionally guided reclamation programs in the West. It was time for a new look. Out of this came the proposal for a National Water Commission and a new champion for conservation in a position powerful enough to make a major difference—Henry M. Jackson, Chairman of the Committee on Interior and Insular Affairs of the Senate. He and his friends used their strength well, and a great remnant of natural America remains unscathed in tribute to their efforts.

With Marble and Bridge Canyon dams blocked, and with public opinion running strongly for saving the Grand Canyon, the logical next step is expanding Grand Canyon National Park to include *all* the Canyon. It is possible, right now, to have a magnificent national park worthy of the magnificence of this place. It is possible, right now, to take the offensive in the name of Grand Canyon; not merely to continue defending it against various perils. It is possible, right now, to guarantee to the American people and to people everywhere that a wild, living, complete Grand Canyon will be a lasting part of mankind's stock of great possessions.

A bill to complete Grand Canyon National Park has already been drafted and introduced to Congress. Compared to what might have been, it is a modest proposal. The easternmost land that could be added to the park is the lower Paria River as it follows the Vermilion Cliffs to join the Colorado at Lee's Ferry (see map at end of this book). Most of this area, including Lee's Ferry, is already under National Park Service management as the southernmost part of the Glen Canyon National Recreation Area.

Adjoining the proposed lower Paria addition on the south (downstream) is the spectacular Marble Gorge section of Grand Canyon. It is an essential part of a larger park as are parts of the adjacent Marble Plain and Vermilion Cliffs to the west. The eastern plain and the Echo Cliffs, however, are part of the Navajo Indian Reservation and would be excluded from the park unless the Navajo Tribal Council decided otherwise. The Navajos have already established tribal parks on their side of Marble Gorge. We should catch up on ours, and we did, part-way, when in January 1969, President Johnson signed a proclamation creating Marble Gorge National Monument. It extends from Lee's Ferry fifty river miles to Nankoweap Creek, the present northeastern corner of Grand Canyon National Park. Included in this area is the site where Marble Canyon Dam was to have blocked the river.

The third new section of the park would take in a strip of the Kaibab Plateau currently administered as the Kaibab National Forest. The eastern portion of this country is a beautiful blend of ponds and meadows, conifers and aspen, at altitudes up to 9,000 feet. The western part would include the complex system of Kanab Creek tributaries: Sowats, Jumpup, Indian Hollow, Snake, Hacks, and Grandma. This addition would touch the now unprotected Colorado River for eleven miles between Tapeats and Kanab creeks.

Slightly downstream from and opposite Kanab is Havasu Canyon, at its upper end called Cataract. The lower end of Havasu with its perennial, turquoise stream, two-hundred foot waterfalls, and Havasupai Indians is already within the national park. The rest of this canyon and a portion of the adjacent Coconino Plateau should be added. Only if side canyons in nearly their entirety are included will it be possible for the new park to protect and interpret the entire geological process that resulted in the Grand Canyon.

Farther westward is Grand Canyon National Monument, established in 1932. As with the new Marble Gorge National Monument, this central section of the Grand Canyon, currently administered by the National Park Service, should be accorded park status. The northern end of the Toroweap Valley that was in the 1932 monument but dropped in 1940 should be reinstated. It is a long hall-like entry to a view at Toroweap Point 3,000 feet straight down to the Colorado. With the approval of the Hualapai Tribal Council it might also be possible to add that portion of the Hualapai Indian Reservation abutting the river on the south to the enlarged park.

The western end of Grand Canyon, Lower Granite Gorge, is at present part of Lake Mead National Recreation Area. Yet the spirit of the place is canyon, not lake. There are many rapids, massive evidences of ancient volcanic activity, the almost totally unvisited side canyons that cut back into the Shivwits Plateau, and the site of Bridge Canyon (Hualapai) Dam. The logical place for Grand Canyon National Park to end and Lake Mead National Recreation Area to begin is at Grand Wash Cliffs where the river becomes a lake and the Canyon an open desert.

This enlarged Grand Canyon National Park would total a little over two million acres, slightly smaller than Yellowstone. It would not be an expensive or difficult park to create. Virtually all the land proposed for addition is already federally owned and managed. This fact, however, is not enough for adequate protection, as the dam controversy of the 1960s proved. National park status, with a new provision voiding and prohibiting all power developments in the reserved area, would make the Canyon as safe as present statutes allow.

Men draw park boundaries, but rivers cut canyons. Questions of nomenclature aside, the Grand Canyon is a single, unbroken unit from Lee's Ferry to Grand Wash Cliffs. You sense it from an airplane; you know it running the river. Yet the present boundaries of Grand Canyon National Park do not do even half-justice to the aesthetic and geological unity of the landscape. Of the 280 river miles that are Grand Canyon, only 73 are presently within the park. The Canyon deserves a complete park. The magnificent gesture of nature in this place should call forth the best that Americans can do for one of their nation's superlative wildernesses.

In the Grand Canyon, Arizona has a natural wonder which, so far as I know, is in kind absolutely unparalleled throughout the rest of the world. I want to ask you to do one thing in connection with it in your own interest and in the interest of the country. . . . Leave it as it is. You cannot improve on it. The ages have been at work on it, and man can only mar it. What you can do is keep it for your children, your children's children, and for all who come after you as one of the great sights which every American . . . can see.

THEODORE ROOSEVELT

The Canyon in Congress

More than once the future of the living Grand Canyon has hung in the balance as men and women debated the issue on the floors and in the committee rooms of Congress. The House Committee on Interior and Insular Affairs has heard a considerable share of testimony on the Grand Canyon; in this excerpt from the official hearings of August 1965, Madelyn Leopold, a high-school student from Washington, D. C., testified before the Subcommittee on Irrigation and Reclamation. Her interlocutors were Representative Walter E. Rogers of Texas and Representative Wayne Aspinall of Colorado, the committee's chairman.—ED.

MR. ROGERS. Miss Leopold, I think you probably qualify as the youngest witness to ever come before the subcommittee. You may have a seat, if you like.

Do you have a written statement?

MISS LEOPOLD. Yes; I do.

My name is Madelyn Leopold. I am testifying as a private citizen, obviously. I go to National Cathedral School. I am going to be a senior this year. I would like to read a statement that I have written, that I would like to have you hear.

My purpose in testifying to you today is merely selfish. For the majority of people, the most obvious reason why these dams should not be built is that they will yield the Southwest a real net loss of water, which would be a ridiculous sacrifice in this chronically arid region. However, I am personally interested in the sacrifice of beauty the erection of these dams would effect, the travesty they would play upon the country's current drive to beautification. I am against the dams because they will create pure ugliness, and I don't want the future generations, or mine, to suffer from your mistake. For those of you who have never seen what a dam can do, I would like to tell you from my own experience.

This summer, I spent a week in a rubber raft floating down the San Juan River to Lake Powell. The river was magnificent in its force and motion. It was clean and alive. The canyon was as breathtaking as any Gothic cathedral, for like a cathedral, it was hundreds of feet high; intricately carved; and splendidly colored by sun, shadows, and white moonlight. Even such a comparatively small canyon was worth missing a trip to Europe.

But Lake Powell was another thing: the water was flat and still, like a lake, yet lacking all the beauty of a lake. It was dirty and littered, the trash lying to rot on the motionless water. The canyon was only about 50 feet high, and the feeling I experienced upon moving from the river into the lake was somewhat like that of going from a cathedral into a bomb shelter. Furthermore, the walls of the canyon were streaked with silt left by the water as it rose and fell, regulated, as it were, by a faucet. Imagine the Colorado River reduced to the mere dimensions of a bathtub. The proposed dams in the Colorado would, in fact, create a similar situation, different only in that they would ruin a more beautiful spectacle.

Furthermore, if you drown the living Colorado, you will eliminate any educational value whatsoever that the canyon today offers to the tourists and their children. Being a student myself, I am very much aware of the effectiveness which a concrete example can have in illustrating a dry textbook fact. Today the canyon is the living scene of history, the very site of great American pioneer exploration. On the San Juan River, when my father spoke of Powell and the first expedition on the Colorado, I really could see the history being relived in the story waters of the river. And the Grand Canyon, too, is the most beautiful example of geological processes now existing on earth. If you drown the river, the creator of the canyon will be extinguished, and the canyon will become only a ludicrous imitation of its former self, no longer a thing of nature, for nature cannot operate with a faucet. For students like myself, and people with a feeling for beauty, the erection of these dams would be a great mistake.

I have discussed this with my classmates and my friends have all said: "How can they do that to the Grand Canyon, of all places? If the public knew about it, the government wouldn't get away with something like that." Among my peers there is a lot of disillusionment with government, but nobody could believe that an elected administration would sink as low as to deface the Grand Canyon. And, of course, the public is uninformed. If Americans knew of this project, they'd be as amazed as my friends. But no one knows. Just yesterday, I saw an article in the July *McCall's* about the Grand Canyon in which the author calls it "not just an American spectacular . . . (but) a true world wonder for all the world's people." How can this administration advocate natural beauty and "see America first" when it seeks to deface that beauty? For your children, and theirs, I would hope that you could leave just this one token of your personal values, that future generations may sigh at the spectacles of Grand Canyon and say to you, "Those Americans knew the value of real beauty." . . .

Mr. Aspinall. Now, let me ask you the $64 question. . . . How many young people, do you think, in the United States will be given the opportunity to take the trip that you have taken?

Miss Leopold. Sir, I cannot really tell. I know of a few—at least a hand-ful—just among my friends who have had the chance to do it and have done it—at least similar things.

Mr. Aspinall. I think what this committee is up against is trying to decide how much space we will leave for young people who are blessed with the back-ground and the family that you have, to enjoy some of the things that you like as compared with those people who will have to take the other.

The issue remains alive as long as the Canyon is threatened. In March 1967, in a session of the same House subcommittee, representatives of the Sierra Club, including David Brower (then executive director of the club) and Jeffrey Ingram, put the case for preserving the Grand Canyon before Representatives Sam Steiger and Morris K. Udall, both of Arizona.—Ed.

Mr. Brower. If you would contemplate what a dam 180 feet higher than the Washington Monument would do to some of the finest sculpture on the river, you would know first that that would never be seen again. It would be underwater. And finally as my testimony shows—and rather sooner than later, possibly—it is perpetually gone under sedimentation. That is major damage to the scenic resource.

Mr. Steiger. The only result would be to reduce the trip from somewhere up around 13 or 14 days to somewhere around 6 or 7 days.

Mr. Brower. I think we will have to disagree on that very strongly.

Mr. Steiger. I wouldn't be surprised if we disagreed. . . .

Mr. Udall. Mr. Brower, maybe we can start out by compromising. I have had no indication that the Sierra Club is ever willing to compromise but . . . I had thought that maybe if we took Marble Canyon out as I am willing to do, and put it in the park as I am willing to do, and give you 158 miles of living river instead of 104 which wasn't sufficient last year, that maybe we had the grounds of compromise.

If we lower the dam so that we take out 13 miles more and we give you 171 miles of living river forever, does the Sierra Club find this proposition at all interesting? . . .

One of the things that has troubled many of my colleagues here is what they deem the impossibly adamant noncompromising position of the Sierra Club. We have 104 miles of living river, the longest stretch of national park in the country. We enlarge that to 158 miles. We are willing to enlarge the Grand Canyon to take in Marble Gorge and Vermilion Cliffs and all of that. We are willing to talk about going downstream another 13 miles. What would the Sierra Club accept? If we have a low, low, low Bridge Canyon Dam, maybe 100 feet high, is that too much? Is there any point at which you compromise here?

Mr. Brower. Mr. Udall, you are not giving us anything that God didn't put there in the first place, and I think that is the thing we are not entitled to compromise. That is the primary scenic resource of this country. If there are no other ways to go about getting your water, I would still say that the compromise should not be made—that Arizona should be subsidized with something other than the world's Grand Canyon, or any part of it.

We would not expect you to sacrifice a major part of the central Arizona aqueduct for the possibility of getting water. You are here for the principle of getting water for Arizona. And although we could question some of the economics of this, we are perfectly willing to compromise there.

The aqueduct is going to damage a great deal of scenery. The new storage reservoirs along the aqueduct will too. These things we are taking a walk on. On the Grand Canyon, we are not entitled to take a walk.

MR. UDALL. You won't agree or compromise on any point regardless of what you conceive to be the total geological Grand Canyon regardless of how high, how low, how little damage or anything else.

MR. INGRAM. I think we are biased by the use of "compromise" as a verb. This is not a compromise. You can't compromise when one side says, "We will define what is to be compromised." Both sides have to come together, and I have been emphasizing this point, of course, as you know, for several months, that you have to come together first and talk about what you can discuss as to compromise. We have never been able to do that. Every time we have come in here we have been accused of being inflexible and not bargaining in good faith issues that are important to us.

MR. UDALL. We know your position and you know ours. What I am getting at, I want the record to show that the Sierra Club would not slacken its efforts in any degree if we lowered the dam by any amount or changed the dam in any way. This is the point I wanted to make. Nor does the Sierra Club slacken its efforts or compromise when the Secretary of the Interior and the administration are willing to simply defer the dam and take five more years to decide whether we build it.

You say that you will continue to fight and try to defeat the bill unless it contains a provision setting aside that damsite once and for all time in the Grand Canyon National Park.

MR. BROWER. We have no choice. There have to be groups who will hold for these things that are not replaceable. If we stop doing that, we might as well stop being an organization, and conservation organizations might as well throw in the towel.

MR. UDALL. I know the strength and sincerity of your feelings, and I respect them.

*The dam builders will always be hynotized by their
desire to exploit the Colorado River and its gorge,
to drain from the river the energy we have felt.
Yet there are other ways of generating electric power.*

There is no other Grand Canyon.

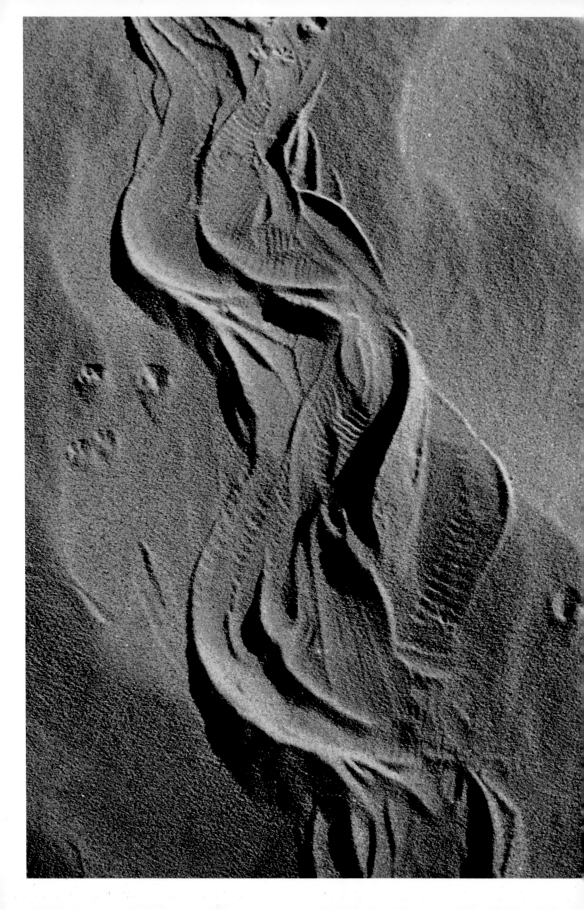

Can we afford to keep some land free of the contrivances of the world we made?
Can we afford places where all we need do is learn to walk easily
through the world we were made in?
Can we afford to set aside national parks? Can we afford not to?
Dams or people? You can help decide.

And if you think some land should be left, exalting its own life;

if you feel that clouds should not have to contend for space with smog;
if you think that somewhere a garden should be able to grow uncultivated;

that a pond should be left to itself, to support its own community;

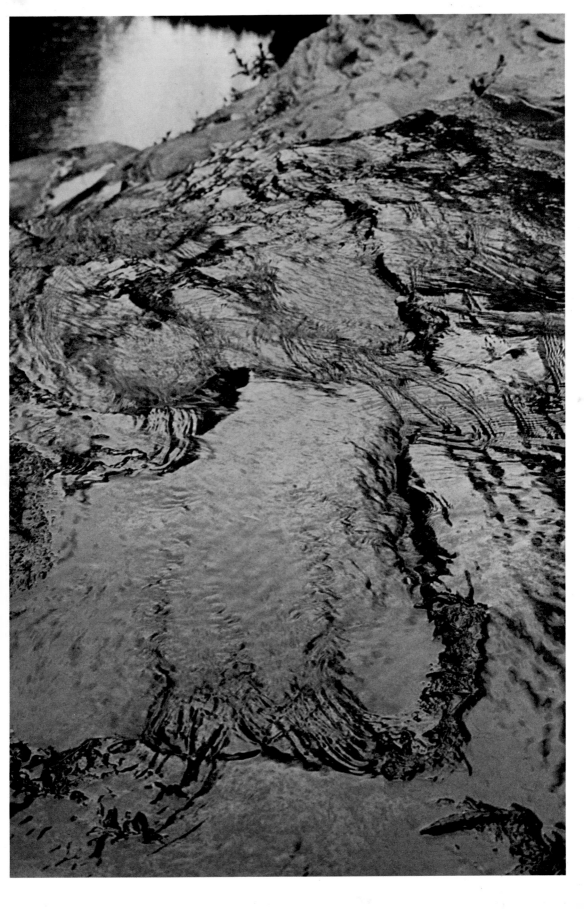

if you are pleased to see a stream running pure, glorifying a natural pavement;
if you are content to enjoy a river shore, leaving its design undisturbed;

if you think a wilderness river should be left dancing, alive and bringing life;

if you have come, even a little, under the spell of this place,
then this canyon we have seen only a little of,
this Grand Canyon,
is your Grand Canyon.

Grand Canyon Battle Ads

DAVID BROWER

THE FIRST full-page advertisement on behalf of the American wilderness came to the aid of the Colorado River system on October 31, 1955, when, through the philanthropy of the late Edward H. Mallinckrodt, Jr., and the public relations genius of Frederick M. Smith, an unusual page appeared in the *Denver Post*. Signed by the Council of Conservationists, it warned sponsors of the Colorado River Storage Project, who were meeting in Denver at the time, that they should abandon plans to build Echo Park and Split Mountain dams in Dinosaur National Monument. The ad made clear that unless these dams were irrevocably deleted from their plans, the wilderness lobby would use every legal means to block passage of the rest of the project. Aware of the power of organized conservationists, and wanting above all to obtain water and power for the Southwest, the sponsors agreed to take the controversial dams out of the bill.

Not until December 1965 was a full-page ad used for a similar conservation end. Representatives of various conservation organizations and foundations were to meet with Secretary of the Interior Stewart L. Udall to discuss the boundaries of a potential Redwood National Park—a long-dormant proposal brought back to life through the leadership of Martin Litton, Edgar Wayburn, François Leydet, and Philip Hyde, whose work helped create the Sierra Club's book, *The Last Redwoods*.

I urged the advertisement as a means of bringing forcibly to the Secretary's and the nation's attention the urgency of protecting as much as possible of the Redwood Creek watershed in that park—an urgency the Secretary's meeting was about to overlook. The ad was run concurrently in five newspapers—*The New York Times, Washington Post, San Francisco Chronicle, Los Angeles Times,* and *Sacramento Bee*. The ad, and almost three years of successful work following it, helped measurably in rescuing part of the superlative forests of Redwood Creek. The Internal Revenue Service demonstrated no concern about the form or vigor of the club's action. The administration favored a Redwood National Park.

By the following June, however, another battle raged in which the administration favored the building of two dams in the Grand Canyon. A series of ads that was to make conservation history was begun. Between June 9, 1966, and April 16, 1967, the Sierra Club placed four full-page ads in *The New York Times* (some of them were repeated in many other newspapers and magazines) to carry forward the battle to keep dams out of the Grand Canyon.

The first of the series was extraordinary in two ways. It was a split run—

something the *Times* had never undertaken before in its daily paper. Half of the June 9 copies of the *Times* contained my relatively quiet open letter to Secretary Udall, asking him to help save Grand Canyon and asking the public to speak up, too. It contained one coupon, addressed to the Sierra Club.

The other version was professionally written, for the most part by Jerry Mander, of the firm of Freeman and Gossage in San Francisco, and it outpulled the amateur ad by about three to two. It contained seven coupons, to be filled in and mailed if the reader could not find time to write individual letters. The coupons were addressed to the President, Secretary Udall, Congressman Wayne Aspinall of the House Interior Committee, to the reader's individual Representative and Senators, and to the Sierra Club. (On this last coupon readers were given the options of contributing money to help the fight, buying a Grand Canyon book, or joining the club.)

The Mander ad brought, in due course, a notable response in coupons sent to Washington and in money sent to the club (enough to cover the cost of the ads). The ad also brought an immediate response from the Internal Revenue Service—a letter, hand-delivered to Sierra Club headquarters in San Francisco the next day, clouding the club's tax-deductible status in such a way as to cut off major contributions to the club at once, an unprecedented application of administrative penalty in advance of investigation. The club submitted a painstaking defense of its position, but the Internal Revenue Service's cursory reply—not delivered until almost two years later—officially affirmed the club's loss of its valuable tax-deductible standing. Redress is at this writing still being sought through the courts and the Congress. The IRS action has cost the club some half million dollars in major contributions.

But there was a concurrent spectacular gain. Small nondeductible contributions multiplied. In three years the membership of the club trebled (from 39,000 in June 1966 to 78,000 in June 1969). And sympathy for the club exploded nationally, in editorials, newspapers and magazine articles, and in the still more convincing route of communication—word of mouth. People who had never heard of the Sierra Club began asking Sierra Club members how the club was getting along with the IRS. And people who had always known about the Grand Canyon but who had been quite unaware of any threat to it were now very much aware of the threat. The further advertisements, in the face of the IRS action, kept the public aware.

Howard Gossage, in the course of the first ad's preparation, said that advertising is not really worth running unless it gets talked about and the reader can do something about it. This one was talked about. The Sierra Club realized it was far more concerned about a canyon than about tax status. And backlash from the IRS intervention was probably one of the important factors in staving off the dams. The American public, it turned out, did not wish the tax man to jeopardize the world's only Grand Canyon.

tric demand. Some days there will only be acres of mud where the flowing river and living canyon now are.

4. Why are these dams being built, then? For commercial power. They are dams of the sort which their sponsor, the Bureau of Reclamation of the Department of the Interior, calls "cash registers."

In other words, these dams aren't even to store water for people and farms, but to provide *auxiliary* power for industry, Arizona power politics in your Grand Canyon.

Moreover, Arizona doesn't need the dams to carry out its water development. Actually, it would have more water without the dams.

5. For, the most remarkable fact is that, as Congressional hearings have confirmed, seepage and evaporation at these remote damsites would annually *lose* enough water to supply both Phoenix and Tucson.

As for the remainder, far more efficient power sources are available right now, and at lower net cost. For the truth is, that the Grand Canyon dams will cost far more than they can earn.

6. Recognizing the threat to Grand Canyon, the Bureau of the Budget (which speaks for the President on such matters) has already suggested a moratorium on one of the dams and proposed a commission consider alternatives.

This suggestion has been steadily resisted by Mr. Aspinall's House Committee, which continues to proceed with H. R. 4671. It has been actively fought by the Bureau of Reclamation.

7. At the same time, interestingly, other Bureaus within Secretary Udall's domain (notably National Parks, Fish and Wildlife, Indian Affairs, Mines, Outdoor Recreation, Geological Survey) have been discouraged from presenting their findings, obtained at public expense. Only the Reclamation Bureau has been heard.

8. Meanwhile, in a matter of days the bill will be on the floor of Congress and—let us make the shocking fact completely clear—it will probably pass.

The only thing that can stop it is your prompt action.

to the Sierra Club; that's us.)

10. Remember, with all the complexities of Washington politics and Arizona politics, and the ins and outs of committees and procedures, there is only one simple, incredible issue here: This time it's the Grand Canyon they want to flood. *The Grand Canyon.*

WHAT THE SIERRA CLUB IS FOR

The Sierra Club, founded in 1892 by John Muir, is nonprofit, supported by people who sense what Thoreau sensed when he wrote, "In wildness is the preservation of the world." The club's program is nationwide, includes wilderness trips, books, and films—and a major effort to protect the remnant of wilderness in the Americas.

There are now twenty chapters, branch offices in New York, Washington, Albuquerque, Seattle, and Los Angeles, and a main office in San Francisco.

This advertisement has been made possible by individual contributions, particularly from our Atlantic, Rocky Mountain, Rio Grande, Southern California and Grand Canyon chapter members, and by buyers of Sierra Club books everywhere, especially the twelve in the highly praised Exhibit Format Series, which includes books on Grand Canyon, Glen Canyon, the Redwoods, the Northern Cascades, Mount Everest, and the Sierra.

David Brower, Executive Director,
Sierra Club
Mills Tower, San Francisco, California.

☐ Please send me more of the details of the battle to save Grand Canyon.

☐ I know how much this sort of constructive protest costs. Here is my donation of $_____ to help you continue your work.

☐ Please send me a copy of "Time and the River Flowing," the famous four-color book by Philip Hyde and François Leyder which tells the whole story of Grand Canyon and the battle to save it. I am enclosing $25.00

☐ I would like to be a member of the Sierra Club. Enclosed is $14.00 for entrance fee and first year's dues.

Name_____
Address_____
City_____ State_____ Zip_____
Note: All contributions and membership dues are deductible.

BEFORE THE VOTE ON H.R. 4671? THANK YOU.
Name_____
Address_____
City_____ State_____ Zip_____

No. 3
REPRESENTATIVE WAYNE ASPINALL
HOUSE OF REPRESENTATIVES
WASHINGTON 25, D.C.
I URGE YOU TO HALT PROCEEDINGS ON H.R. 4671, NOW IN YOUR COMMITTEE, AND TO SEEK EXPERT TESTIMONY FROM THE MANY INTERIOR DEPARTMENT AGENCIES THAT HAVE NOT YET APPEARED BEFORE YOU. THANK YOU.

Name_____
Address_____
City_____ State_____ Zip_____

No. 4 (To your Congressman)
REPRESENTATIVE _____
HOUSE OF REPRESENTATIVES
WASHINGTON 25, D.C.
PLEASE JOIN IN THE FIGHT TO SAVE GRAND CANYON BY URGING DELETION OF BOTH DAMS PROPOSED IN H.R. 4671. THANK YOU.

Name_____
Address_____
City_____ State_____ Zip_____

No. 5 (To one of your U.S. Senators)
SENATOR _____
UNITED STATES SENATE
WASHINGTON 25, D.C.
PLEASE JOIN IN THE FIGHT TO SAVE GRAND CANYON BY URGING DELETION OF BOTH DAMS PROPOSED IN H.R. 4671. THANK YOU.

Name_____
Address_____
City_____ State_____ Zip_____

No. 6 (To your state's other Senator)
SENATOR _____
UNITED STATES SENATE
WASHINGTON 25, D.C.
PLEASE JOIN IN THE FIGHT TO SAVE GRAND CANYON BY URGING DELETION OF BOTH DAMS PROPOSED IN H.R. 4671. THANK YOU.

Name_____
Address_____
City_____ State_____ Zip_____

(If they can turn Grand Canyon into a "cash register"
is any national park safe? You know the answer.)

Now Only You Can Save Grand Canyon From Being Flooded... For Profit

Yes, that's right, Grand Canyon!
The facts are these:

1. Bill H.R. 4671 is now before Rep. Wayne Aspinall's (Colo.) House Committee on Interior and Insular Affairs. This bill provides for two dams—Bridge Canyon and Marble Gorge—which would stop the Colorado River and flood water back into the canyon.

2. Should the bill pass, two standing lakes will fill what is presently 130 miles of canyon gorge. As for the wild, running Colorado River, the canyon's sculptor for 25,000,000 years, it will become dead water.

3. In some places the canyon will be submerged five hundred feet deep. "The most revealing single page of the earth's history," as Joseph Wood Krutch has described the fantastic canyon walls, will be drowned.

The new artificial shoreline will fluctuate on hydroelec-

U. S. Bureau of Reclamation

The Grand Canyon: How man plans to improve it. (Newsweek, May 30, 1966)

9. What to do? Letters and wires are effective, and so are the forms at right once you have signed them and mailed them. (You will notice that there is also one in the box below

PLEASE CLIP THESE AND MAIL THEM

No. 1
THE PRESIDENT
THE WHITE HOUSE
WASHINGTON 25, D.C.

THANK YOU FOR YOUR STAND, THROUGH THE BUREAU OF THE BUDGET, PROTECTING GRAND CANYON. WOULD YOU PLEASE ASK CONGRESS TO DEFER BOTH GRAND CANYON DAMS PENDING INVESTIGATION OF THE ALTERNATE POWER SOURCES. THANK YOU AGAIN.

Name _____
Address _____
City _____ State _____ Zip _____

No. 2

SECRETARY OF THE INTERIOR STEWART UDALL
WASHINGTON 25, D.C.

ALL YOUR SPLENDID CONSERVATION WORK OF THE PAST WILL BE BLIGHTED IF YOU ALLOW THE LIVING GRAND CANYON TO DIE AT THE HANDS OF YOUR BUREAU OF RECLAMATION. WOULD YOU PLEASE ALLOW THE FINDINGS OF YOUR OTHER BUREAUS TO BE REPORTED FULLY TO CONGRESS

Dear Mr. Udall:

If Congress lets your Reclamation Bureau ruin Grand Canyon with two dams, can any national park be safe?

Your Reclamation engineers, if you give them a chance, will kill the river that created Grand Canyon and is still creating it. They will flood out 130 miles of the living Colorado (they have already done this to 600 miles of it), shunt more of it through a tunnel, drown or shrivel the oases along the river's edge – vital to wildlife, important to America's natural beauty, and essential to people who like what Grand Canyon is.

The Bureau wants to build these dams to make money. The same Bureau has threatened the National Park System whenever its Secretary let it. The Bureau people talk about water for Arizona. But they waste water. Their obsolete methods already evaporate enough of the Colorado River to supply two or three Denvers, and now they want to waste enough more for Phoenix and your Tucson.

1902 Bureau methods don't add up in 1966

You remember our proving how bad their arithmetic about reservoir evaporation was a few years ago – how in the Echo Park battle they were awarded a rubber slide rule for stretching the truth.

They are still at it. Now they claim they need two cash-register dams (their term) in Grand Canyon. They don't. This is their way to finance pumping water to Arizona from an existing reservoir and to take water from the Columbia River, much of it for southern California.

But accurate arithmetic has proved before the House Interior Committee (in spite of an attempt to block conservation testimony) that the dams really aren't the way to help the Southwest. They are simply the Bureau way, the 1902 way in an atomic age the Bureau can't quite face.

Who really pays? A good question

To build their dams, the Bureau people want to borrow a billion-odd dollars from the Treasury, pay enormously less interest than the Treasury itself pays to get the money, and promise to repay most of their debt out of revenues from Hoover and Parker and Davis dams after paying what they still owe on them. They probably wouldn't want Price-Waterhouse or Dun & Bradstreet to check them out. We would. For the Bureau's own figures,

After Reclamation ruins Grand Canyon, then what?

Mr. Secretary, suppose you let your Bureau ruin Grand Canyon with dams. What would the Bureau do for an encore?

Projections show that the dams would satisfy the Southwest's growing appetite for power for only three years, if that. Let's imagine Grand Canyon dammed and its river dead, your fellow Arizonans would have to look right away for new sources of power, and would find them.

Too late. The Bureau's kind of blind planning has now destroyed Glen Canyon, just upstream from Grand Canyon to produce electricity – power that will be available cheaper from alternate sources before Glen Canyon reservoir is half full.

So why not skip Grand Canyon dams and start with the encore? Why not start with the alternatives and strike a useful blow for sound planning, not a low blow at Grand Canyon?

You will remember what Theodore Roosevelt said about the Canyon in 1903: "Leave it as it is. You cannot improve on it. The ages have been at work on it and man can only mar it." We, and Arizonans (some of them secretly), know he was right.

The living river still counts

Time and the river flowing – these created the Grand Canyon. The exquisite sculpture of stone two billion years old is now being revealed in the inner gorges as the river turns the pages it has been turning for twenty-five million years. The artificial lakes your Reclamation Bureau would back up behind the dams, in their own compulsion to invade the National Park System and to kill wild rivers, will cover the finest Grand Canyon pages with mud. A living river – nothing else – can keep the Canyon alive to tell its ageless story.

In five years your Reclamation engineers can close the Grand Canyon show – the essence and excellence of it – end it for all our civilization's time.

Won't you please find them something better to do?

Sincerely,

David Brower,
Executive Director, Sierra Club

You can help save Grand Canyon. You are unique, possessed of your own brand of genius and of the power to do what counts.

You remember what Rachel Carson did to prevent pesticides from ushering in a silent spring, what Ralph Nader is doing to make cars safe, what people you know have achieved who do their homework, who care, and who stand up to be counted.

Your letters—especially your follow-up— will make the difference.

The prediction is that Mr. Aspinall's House Interior Committee will soon act to bring the Lower Colorado River development legislation (H.R. 4671) to the House floor for vote. Now is the time to express your wish—if it is your wish—by asking your own Congressman to insist that the Grand Canyon dams be deleted from this legislation and that alternatives be found to save money, and, above all, to spare Grand Canyon. Don't be satisfied with the all-too-frequent reply—the Bureau's self-serving statement.

If you care enough, you can do something no one else can do—write in your own way, soon, to the men listed below.

The President, The White House

The Honorable Stewart L. Udall

Your two Senators, Senate Office Building

Your Representative, House Office Building

(All are in Washington, D. C.; your postmaster can supply missing names and zip codes.)

If you will, write us too and let us know how you made out.

What the Sierra Club is for

The Sierra Club, founded in 1892 by John Muir, is nonprofit, supported by people who sense what Thoreau sensed when he wrote, "In wildness is the preservation of the world." The club's program is nationwide, includes wilderness trips, books, and films—and a major effort to protect the remnant of wilderness in the Americas.

There are now twenty-odd chapters, branch offices in New York, Washington, Albuquerque, Seattle, and Los Angeles, and a main office in San Francisco. Annual dues, $9; admission fee, $5; further generosity is all right.

This advertisement has been made possible by individual contributions, particularly from our Atlantic, Rocky Mountain, Rio Grande, and Grand Canyon chapter members, and by buyers of Sierra Club books everywhere, especially the twelve in the highly praised Exhibit Format Series, which includes books on Grand Canyon, Glen Canyon, the Redwoods, the Northern Cascades, Mount Everest, and even the Sierra.

After all, it's the Grand Canyon. That's enough for us. We hope it's enough for you.

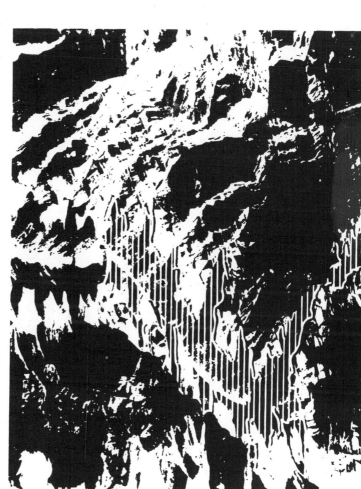

1) A bill will soon be voted in Congress (H.R. 4671) which would put two dams into Grand Canyon, maiming for all time the wild river that has been the canyon's sculptor for 25,000,000 years.

2) If the bill passes, two artificial lakes will back up into 133 miles of canyon gorge. And hardly a century later, silting will have created wall to wall mud and tangled growth.

3) In some places, the inner gorge will be submerged five hundred feet. A vital part of "The most revealing single page of the earth's history," as Joseph Wood Krutch has described it, will be drowned.

4) It is argued that artificial lakes will be an "improvement" because tourists will be nearer the walls.

Should we flood the Sistine Chapel, so tourists can float nearer the ceiling?

5) Between the lakes, the Colorado's depth will vary fifteen feet from day to day, depending on hydroelectric demand.

Shoreline campsites will become suddenly dangerous. Wildlife will be disrupted, as will the ecology of one of history's treasures.

There is no part of the Colorado River within Grand Canyon that would not be affected.

6) The dams will not be used for water. They are expected to make money by sale of commercial power.

7) But for even the making of money, Grand Canyon dams will soon be as obsolete as they are unnecessary. Congressional testimony established they are fantastically expensive and wasteful of water. Still the alternatives are ignored.

8) The real push for the dams is political—an attempt by the seven states in the Colorado Basin to finance diversion of water from the Columbia River to the Colorado, at a cost of an undetermined number of billions of dollars to the other states.

9) If the bill does pass, no national park will be safe. With the unthinkable precedent set in Grand Canyon, it will be simple to approve dams or other commercial projects *already proposed* in a dozen national parks.

10) If the bill passes, America will have violated a treaty obligation signed at the International Convention on Nature Protection and Wildlife Preservation, that it would never subject a national park to exploitation for commercial profit.

Our entire National Park System, so brilliant it has been a model for every nation in the world, would suddenly be meaningless.

11) Secretary of the Interior Stewart Udall could do much to save the day.

Taking advantage of the important new evidence presented in the House hearings, he could urge the dams be deleted from H.R. 4671. He could urge that Congressional committees at least hear the findings of his National Park Service, Bureaus of Recreation, and Mines and Geological Survey, instead of only Reclamation.

By failure to act, Mr. Udall is assisting the demise of the great park system he was pledged to protect.

12) It is an accident of history, but it is this generation which must assure that something untrammeled and free remains in the American earth as testimony that we had love for the people who follow.

13) It is for all the above reasons that we ran the two advertisements on June 9th—protesting the destruction of Grand Canyon—that produced an unprecedented reaction by the Internal Revenue Service.

By 4 P.M. the next day, an IRS messenger delivered a letter to us in San Francisco. It cast a cloud over our tax deductible status, effectively stopping major financial assistance for our public service program.

IRS read the ads as a sudden attempt to "influence legislation" in a "substantial" way. (They do not define those terms, leaving organizations like ours at the mercy of administrative whim.) *And they do not even raise the question with organizations that favor the dams.*

14) The Sierra Club has been in the business of helping people enjoy and save natural beauty for 74 years. Nothing new has been added to this goal in that time, except that the battle to save Grand Canyon is now in its critical phase.

If the IRS succeeds in slowing us down, it will also have slowed every organization which chooses to work for the saving of our resources. And this is no time to slow down.

15) Therefore, tax deductible or not, we intend to continue. After all, as astonishing as it may seem, *it is* the Grand Canyon that's in danger this time. *The Grand Canyon.*

16) Possibly within the next two weeks, the House Committee on Interior and Insular Affairs will have reported out the bill and it will be ready for a floor vote in the House.

You can stop it by adding your coupons to those that have been sent already, or better still, your own letters.

And while we cannot now promise that any contributions you send us are deductible, a determination still in the hands of IRS, we *can* promise that the funds will help fight the remaining battles against a technology that feels it is no longer needs nature.

WHAT THE SIERRA CLUB IS FOR

The Sierra Club, founded in 1892 by John Muir, is nonprofit, supported by people who sense what Thoreau sensed when he wrote, "In wildness is the preservation of the world." The club's program is nationwide, includes wilderness trips, books, and films—and a major effort to protect the remnant of wilderness in the Americas.

There are now twenty chapters, branch offices in New York, Washington, Seattle, and Los Angeles, and a main office in San Francisco.

This advertisement has been made possible by individual contributions, particularly from our Atlantic, Rocky Mountain, Rio Grande, Southern California and Grand Canyon chapter members, and by buyers of Sierra Club books everywhere, especially the twelve in the highly praised Exhibit Format Series, which includes books on Grand Canyon, Glen Canyon, the Redwoods, the Northern Cascades, Mount Everest, and the Sierra.

David Brower, Executive Director
The Sierra Club
Room 1050
Mills Tower Building
San Francisco, California

☐ Please send me more of the details of the battle to save Grand Canyon.

☐ I know how much this sort of constructive protest costs. Here is my donation of $_____ to help you continue your work.

☐ Please send me a copy of "Time and the River Flowing," the famous four-color book by Philip Hyde and Francois Leydet which tells the whole story of Grand Canyon and the battle to save it. I am enclosing $25.00.

☐ I would like to be a member of the Sierra Club. Enclosed is $14.00 for entrance fee and first year's dues.

Name

Address

City ___ State ___ Zip

270 FT.

Vasey's Paradise at Marble Gorge, where a fantastic natural spring gushes out of the rock canyon wall, will be submerged, 270 feet of water. The Statue of Liberty and its base, placed at this spot, would have only its upper arm and torch showing above the water. If the dams are built in Grand Canyon, 133 miles of inner gorge will be submerged by water as deep as 500 feet, and later by that much mud.

Dinosaur and Big Bend, Glacier and
Grand Teton, Kings Canyon,
Redwoods, Mammoth, Even Yellowstone
and Yosemite. And
The Wild Rivers, and Wilderness.

How Can You Guarantee These, Mr. Udall,
If Grand Canyon Is Dammed For Profit?

No. 1

THE PRESIDENT
THE WHITE HOUSE
WASHINGTON 25, D.C.

PLEASE ASK CONGRESS TO DEFER
BOTH GRAND CANYON DAMS
PENDING INVESTIGATION OF THE
ALTERNATE SOURCES OF FUNDS.
HELP SAVE OUR NATIONAL PARKS.
THANK YOU.

Name_____

Address_____

City_____

State_____   Zip_____

No. 2

SECRETARY OF THE INTERIOR
STEWART UDALL
WASHINGTON 25, D.C.

ALL YOUR SPLENDID CONSERVA-
TION WORK OF THE PAST WILL BE
BLIGHTED IF YOU ALLOW THE
LIVING GRAND CANYON TO DIE AT
THE HANDS OF YOUR BUREAU OF
RECLAMATION. WOULD YOU PLEASE
REPORT FULLY TO CONGRESS ON
THE FINDINGS OF YOUR OTHER
BUREAUS, BEFORE THE VOTE ON
H.R. 4671? THANK YOU.

Name_____

Address_____

City_____

State_____   Zip_____

No. 3

SENATOR HENRY M. JACKSON,
CHAIRMAN, SENATE COMMITTEE ON
INTERIOR AND INSULAR AFFAIRS
SENATE OFFICE BUILDING
WASHINGTON 25, D.C.

WHEN YOU BEGIN HEARINGS ON
H.R. 4671, I URGE YOU TO COMPLETE
THE RECORD BY SEEKING EXPERT
TESTIMONY FROM THE MANY
INTERIOR DEPARTMENT AGENCIES
THAT WERE NEVER ASKED TO
APPEAR BEFORE THE HOUSE
COMMITTEE. THANK YOU.

Name_____

Address_____

City_____

State_____   Zip_____

No. 4

(To your Congressman)
REPRESENTATIVE_____
HOUSE OF REPRESENTATIVES
WASHINGTON 25, D.C.

PLEASE JOIN IN THE FIGHT TO
SAVE GRAND CANYON BY URGING
DELETION OF BOTH DAMS PRO-
POSED IN H.R. 4671. THANK YOU.

Name_____

Address_____

City_____

State_____   Zip_____

No. 5

(To one of your U.S. Senators)
SENATOR_____
UNITED STATES SENATE
WASHINGTON 25, D.C.

PLEASE JOIN IN THE FIGHT TO
SAVE GRAND CANYON BY URGING
DELETION OF BOTH DAMS PRO-
POSED IN H.R. 4671. THANK YOU.

Name_____

Address_____

City_____

State_____   Zip_____

No. 6

(To your state's other Senator)
SENATOR_____
UNITED STATES SENATE
WASHINGTON 25, D.C.

PLEASE JOIN IN THE FIGHT TO
SAVE GRAND CANYON BY URGING
DELETION OF BOTH DAMS PRO-
POSED IN H.R. 4671. THANK YOU.

Name_____

Address_____

City_____

State_____   Zip_____

Tourist recreation, as a reason for the dams, is in fact an afterthought. The Bureau of Reclamation, which has backed them, has called the dams "cash registers." It expects the dams would make money by sale of commercial power.

They will not provide anyone with water.

2) In Northern California, four lumber companies have nearly completed logging the private virgin redwood forests, an operation which to give you an idea of its size, has taken fifty years.

Where nature's tallest living things have stood silently since the age of the dinosaurs, much further cutting could make creation of a redwood national park absurd.

The companies have said tourists want only enough roadside trees for the snapping of photos. They offered to spare trees for this purpose, and not much more. The result would remind you of the places on your face you missed while you were shaving.

3) And up the Hudson, there are plans for a power complex —a plant, transmission lines, and a reservoir near and on Storm King Mountain—effectively destroying one of the last wild and high and beautiful spots near New York City.

4) A proposal to flood a region in Alaska as large as Lake Erie would eliminate at once the breeding grounds of more wildlife than conservationists have preserved in history.

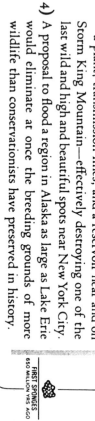

BIRTH OF THE EARTH 4 BILLION YRS AGO

FIRST SPONGES 650 MILLION YRS AGO

FIRST CORALS 575 MILLION YRS AGO

GRAND CANYON 550 MILLION YRS AGO

FIRST FISHES 400 MILLION YRS AGO

---

*The previous ads, urging that readers exercise a constitutional right of petition, to save Grand Canyon, produced an unprecedented reaction by the Internal Revenue Service threatening our tax deductible status. IRS says the ads may be a "substantial" effort to "influence legislation." Undefined, these terms leave organizations like ours at the mercy of administrative whim. (The question has not been raised with any organizations that favor Grand Canyon dams.) So we cannot now promise that contributions you send us are deductible—pending results of what may be a long legal battle.

The Sierra Club, founded in 1892 by John Muir, is nonprofit, supported by people who, like Thoreau, believe "In wildness is the preservation of the world." The club's program is nationwide, includes wilderness trips, books and films — as well as such efforts as this to protect the remnant of wilderness in the Americas. There are now twenty chapters, branch offices in New York (Biltmore Hotel), Washington (Dupont Circle Building), Los Angeles (Auditorium Building), Albuquerque, Seattle, and main office in San Francisco.

☐ ☐ Please send me more details on how I may help.
Here is a donation of $_____ to continue your effort to keep the public informed.

☐ Send me "Time and the River Flowing," famous four color book which tells the complete story of Grand Canyon, and why T. Roosevelt said, "leave it as it is." ($25.00)

☐ Send me "The Last Redwoods" which tells the complete story of the opportunity as well as the destruction in the redwoods. ($17.50)

☐ I would like to be a member of the Sierra Club. Enclosed is $14.00 for entrance and first year's dues.

Name_____

Address_____

City_____ State_____ Zip_____

SHOULD WE ALSO FLOOD THE SISTINE CHAPEL SO TOURISTS CAN GET NEARER THE CEILING?

EARTH began four billion years ago and Man two million. The Age of Technology, on the other hand, is hardly a hundred years old, and on our time chart we have been generous to give it even the little line we have.

It seems to us hasty, therefore, during this blip of time, for Man to think of directing his fascinating new tools toward altering irrevocably the forces which made him. Nonetheless, in these few brief years among four billion, wilderness has all but disappeared. And now these:

1) There are proposals before Congress to "improve" Grand Canyon. Two dams would back up artificial lakes into 148 miles of canyon gorge. This would benefit tourists in power boats, it is argued, who would enjoy viewing the canyon wall more closely. (See headline). Submerged underneath the tourists would be part of the most revealing single page of earth's history. The lakes would be as deep as 600 feet (deeper for example, than all but a handful of New York buildings are high) but in a century, silting would have replaced the water with that much mud, wall to wall.

There is no part of the wild Colorado River, the Grand Canyon's sculptor, that would not be maimed.

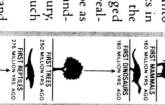

| FIRST MAN 2 MILLION YRS AGO |
| AGE OF TECHNOLOGY |
| FIRST ELEPHANTS 60 MILLION YRS AGO |
| FIRST REDWOODS 130 MILLION YRS AGO |
| FIRST MAMMALS 160 MILLION YRS AGO |
| FIRST DINOSAURS 180 MILLION YRS AGO |
| FIRST TREES 250 MILLION YRS AGO |
| FIRST REPTILES 275 MILLION YRS AGO |

5) In San Francisco, real estate interests have for years been filling a bay that made the city famous, putting tract houses over the fill; and now there's a new idea—still more fill, enough for an air cargo terminal as big as Manhattan.

There exists today a mentality which can conceive such destruction, giving commerce as ample reason. For 74 years, the Sierra Club (now with 46,000 members) has opposed that mentality. But now, when even Grand Canyon is endangered, we are at a critical moment in time.

This generation will decide if something untrammelled and free remains, as testimony we had love for those who follow.

We have been taking ads, therefore, asking people to write their Congressmen and Senators; Secretary of the Interior Stewart Udall; The President; and to send us funds to continue the battle. Thousands *have* written, but meanwhile, Grand Canyon legislation still stands a chance of passage. More letters are needed and much more money, to help fight the notion that Man no longer needs nature.*

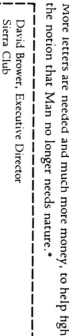

David Brower, Executive Director
Sierra Club
Mills Tower, San Francisco

A number of special interest groups are *still* planning to push dam bills through Congress (and several have already been submitted): Or, failing that, Arizona could build them itself—with or without Administration support.

The key advocates of Grand Canyon dams are these:

1) Commercial interests within the Colorado Basin states, who see these dams (commonly called "cash registers") as a hypothetical means of financing an altogether different project: the turning of part of the Columbia River southward, benefiting themselves, particularly California.

The Grand Canyon itself is of no interest; it is merely an expedient.

2) Southern California real estate developers also gain from presumed dam revenues. (They would like to create still more of Los Angeles.)

3) And the Arizona Power Authority favors the dams. It contends they will provide cheap new sources of power to subsidize Arizona agriculture. (Two-thirds of Arizona's water goes to cattlefeed and cotton, *already* subsidized products.)

The dams will not provide anyone with water. In fact, through seepage and evaporation they will waste enough water to supply Phoenix.

So in summary, while the President's action is heartening, and the Grand Canyon struggle is beginning to turn, we remain in the same essential position, and that is this:

There exists today a mentality which condones destruction done in the name of commerce.

Commercial interests claim we who love the land refuse their "reasonable compromises." But it is forgotten that nearly the whole natural landscape has *already* been compromised . . . tract houses creep over the hillsides, concrete covers the landscape, forests are gone, waters are fouled, and even the air is heavy with waste.

It is not much to ask that some things at least be left "unimproved" to show we have love for those who follow.

If we can't even save Grand Canyon for them, is there hope for saving whatever else of nature our planet still offers?

We have been taking ads, therefore, suggesting that there is something one can do. Thousands have already responded by writing letters (especially important), sending coupons, and also funds to continue the effort; and prospects have thereby improved. But as Grand Canyon legislation still stands a good chance of passage, please don't stop now.

Thank you.

THE GRAND CANYON

The Grand Canyon, measured along the Colorado River that created it, is 280 miles long, and includes Grand Canyon National Park (shown in black), Grand Canyon National Monument (dark grey), and the large surrounding Grand Canyon region (light grey) that is currently unprotected. (The river is shown in white.)

The proposed Hualapai Dam (A) would raise the water level at that point by 659 feet; or by 354 feet more than the height of the Statue of Liberty and its base. (See inset.)

Water will back up all the way to Kanab Creek (B) 93 miles upstream, effectively flooding most of the inner gorge to that point and some of the most elaborate exhibits of natural history in the world. Furthermore, within about 100 years, silting will have replaced even this water with that much mud.

The upstream Marble Canyon Dam (C) would back water into an equally spectacular region of Grand Canyon, located above the park, all the way to Lee's Ferry (D). Furthermore, it would release river water irregularly according to hydroelectric demand, so that daily, the river would rise and fall as much as 13 feet, destroying natural exhibits, making river travelling prohibitively dangerous and leaving, where the river bank had been, a wasteland where nothing will grow.

"Grand Canyon National Monument Is Hereby Abolished"

—From a bill submitted to Congress 15 days ago by Rep. Wayne Aspinall

Had You Thought The Battle Against Dams In Grand Canyon Was Over?

I "GOLIATH AND THE PHILISTINES"

ON FEBRUARY 1, Secretary of the Interior Stewart Udall, speaking for the Administration, announced that the President had withdrawn all support for the Marble Canyon Dam, which would have altered irrevocably the wild Colorado River and ruined a large part of Grand Canyon. In fact, the Secretary reported, the Administration was now advocating expansion of Grand Canyon National Park to *include* this dam site (see map).

A great victory, everyone felt, and the Sierra Club offices were inundated with wires, letters, flowers, and pleasant encomiums praising us, as one note said, "for having slain Goliath and turned away the Philistines."

Naturally enough, most people assumed the *whole* struggle was over. But, as usual, it is not so simple. By now, we have several "Goliaths" and as for the Philistines, they're coming back over the hill.

II "CASH REGISTERS"

FOR while we can now look forward to Administration support, this must be understood:

III TOURISTS IN POWER BOATS

SUPPORTERS of the dams suggest that building them in Grand Canyon is only good sense.

They point out that the new "recreational lakes" will benefit tourists in power boats who will enjoy viewing the upper canyon walls more closely.

Should we flood the Sistine Chapel, so tourists can get nearer the ceiling?

And, to express their "willingness to compromise," some of the dam builders have lately suggested just one dam in Grand Canyon instead of two. Like one bullet in the heart instead of two. (The point, you see, is that if you alter the river's flow at *any* point you interfere with the life force of the canyon, the element which has made it what writers have called "a museum of the history of the world.")

In some quarters, even Mr. Aspinall's bill (see headline) is considered a "compromise," as it would extend Grand Canyon National *Park* upstream while eliminating Grand Canyon National *Monument* (to make room for a 93 mile reservoir). It is felt that if what you are flooding is no longer part of the park system, the public will no longer think it important.

But changing official names around doesn't change the fact that it is all part of Grand Canyon, and once flooded, whatever is under the water is gone forever.

IV MENTALITY

No. 1

The President
The White House
Washington 25, D.C.

Dear Mr. President:

I wish to congratulate you for your Administration's position opposing the Marble Canyon Dam and the suggestion that Grand Canyon National Park be extended upstream.

However, I am still concerned that the Hualapai Dam may be built *downstream*, thereby flooding 93 miles of canyon gorge and marring forever what Joseph Wood Krutch described as "the most revealing single page of the Earth's history . . ." . . . therefore that you speak out at . . . carefully . . . that no special interest groups be able to push a bill containing it through Congress.

Yours sincerely,

Address

City _____ State _____ Zip _____

No. 2

Hon. Wayne Aspinall, Chairman
House Committee on Interior and Insular Affairs
House Office Building
Washington 25, D.C.

Dear Mr. Aspinall:

As I am irrevocably opposed to the sacrifice of *any* part of Grand Canyon to commercial interests, I therefore urge that you reconsider your oft-stated support for proposals to dam Grand Canyon.

Testimony has proven that dams are completely unnecessary, even wasteful, and that alternate power sources are available. And new testimony is also available substantiating that Grand Canyon dams are unneeded.

. . . urge that your committee invite *this* testimony and consider it carefully, and I urge that you refrain from backing these dam bills.

Yours sincerely,

Address

City _____ State _____ Zip _____

No. 3

Hon. John Saylor
House Committee on Interior and Insular Affairs
House Office Building
Washington 25, D.C.

Dear Mr. Saylor:

I congratulate you for your forthright opposition to efforts which would push through your committee legislation which could ultimately wreck our entire National Park System.

Your voice has been among the bravest and most effective in the anti-dam struggle and I would like you to know there are many of us

GRAND CANYON RIVER MILES

Lee's Ferry to Temple Bar

Major rapids in italics
R—right bank; L—left bank

Place	Mile
Lee's Ferry (elev. 3115)	0
3 Mile Wash (from R)	2.8
4 Mile Wash (from L)	4
5 Mile Wash (from L)	5.1
Start of Marble Gorge . . . . approx.	5.3
Navajo Bridge (467 feet above river) .	5.5
6 Mile Wash (from R)	5.7
Badger Creek (from R) and	
Rapid 12.5′ drop	7.9
10 Mile Rock	10
Soap Creek Rapid (from R) 16′ drop .	11.2
Brown's Rock Inscription (on L)	12
A first night camp (on L)	12.5
Sheer Wall Canyon (from L)	
and Rapid, 9.5′ drop	14.4
House Rock Canyon (from R)	
and Rapid, 9′ drop	17
18 Mile Wash (from L), elev. 2997 . .	18.2
Boulder Narrows	18.5
19 Mile Canyon (from R)	19
North Canyon (from R) and	
Rapid, 12′ drop	20.6
21 Mile Rapid	21.3
22 Mile Wash (from L)	21.5
24 Mile Rapid, 4.8′ drop	24.2
Tanner Wash (from L)	24.5
24½ Mile Rapid, 8.2′ drop	24.5
25 Mile Rapid, 6′ drop	25
Cave Springs Rapid, 5′ drop	25.5
27 Mile Rapid, 7′ drop	26.7
Elevation is 2900′	27.7
29 Mile Canyon (from L)	
and Rapid, 6′ drop	29.2
Paradise Canyon (from R)	
and Rapid	31.7
Vasey's Paradise (on R)	31.9
Redwall Cavern (on L)	33
36 Mile Rapid, 8′ drop	36.1
Site of proposed Marble	
Canyon Dam . . . . approx.	38
South Canyon (from R)	
and Loper's Boat	40.9
Royal Arches (on R)	41.3
President Harding Rapid	43.7
Triple Alcoves (on R)	46.5
Saddle Canyon (from R)	47.2
National Park Boundary, elev. 2800′ . .	49.4
Little Nankoweap (from R)	52
Big Nankoweap (from R)	
and Rapid, 14′ drop	52.3
Kwagunt Canyon (from R)	
and *Rapid*, 6′ drop	56
Malgosa Canyon (from R)	57.6
Awatubi Canyon (from R)	58.2
60 Mile Canyon (from R)	
and Rapid, 5′ drop	59.7
Little Colorado River (from L)	
elev. 2713′	61.4
Carbon Canyon (from R)	64.6
Tanner Mine	65.2
Lava Canyon (from R)	
and Rapid, 7.8′ drop	65.5
Tanner Canyon (from L) and Rapid .	68.5
Basalt Creek (from R)	69.3
Cardenas Creek (from L)	71.2
Unkar Creek (from R)	
and *Rapid*, 21′ drop	72.5
75 *Mile* Canyon (from L)	
and *Rapid*, 16′ drop	75.4
Red Canyon (from L)	
and *Hance Rapid*, 27′ drop	76.7
Mineral Canyon (from L)	77.8
Asbestos Canyon (from R)	78
Hance Creek (from L)	78.5
Sockdologer Rapid, 19′ drop	78.5
Cottonwood Creek (from L)	
elev. 2498′	80.5
Vishnu Creek (from R)	81.1
Grapevine Creek (from L)	
and *Rapid*, 16′ drop	81.5
83 Mile Canyon (from R)	
and Rapid, 6.8′ drop	83.5
Clear Creek (from R) and Rapid	84
Zoroaster Canyon (from R)	
and Rapid, 7.5′ drop	84.6
Suspension Bridge	87.6
Phantom Ranch and Bright Angel	
Trail area, elev. 2425′	87.7
Garden Creek (from L), sometimes	
called Pipe Creek)	89
Horn Creek (from L)	
and *Rapid*, 6.5′ drop	90.3
Trinity Creek (from R)	91.6
Salt Creek (from L) and Rapid	92.5
Monument Creek (from L)	93.5
Granite Falls Rapid, 17′ drop	93.5
Hermit Creek (from L)	
and *Rapid*, 15′ drop	94.9
Boucher Creek (from L)	
and Rapid, 12.4′ drop	96.6

142]

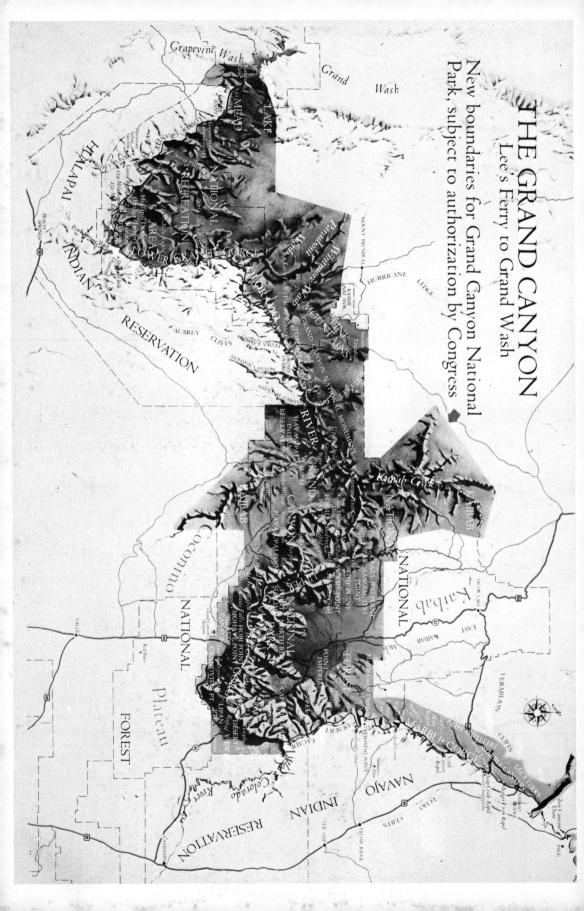